A RAGBAG OF RICHES

An assortment of wordy delights

Collected by

JAMES CHILTON

With illustrations by Kathryn Lamb

Also by James Chilton:

The Last Blue Mountain

ISBN: Paperback 978-1-912262-53-3
ebook 978-1-912262-54-0

Designed, edited and typeset by Alex Chilton
Cover design by Alex Chilton

Published by Clink Street Publishing
Typeset in Classical Garamond

A RAGBAG OF RICHES

An assortment of wordy delights

Collected by

JAMES CHILTON

With illustrations by Kathryn Lamb

ALWAYS MARRY AN APRIL GIRL

Praise the spells and bless the charms,
I found April in my arms.
April golden, April cloudy.
Gracious, cruel, tender, rowdy;
April soft in flowered langour,
April cold with sudden anger,
Ever changing, ever true –
I love April. I love you.

Ogden Nash (1902-1971), American humorous poet.
14 published volumes

For Maggie, an April girl

Contents

Introduction

This collection revives the neglected form of the commonplace book and covers about fifty years from when I was about twenty years old. I squirrelled away quips and quotes before this, but they disappeared in that break with home that comes with adulthood. Some of these entries may be familiar but I have tried to exclude those worn thin by use.

It is a haphazard collection: the Ragbag covering the rougher, even vulgar (but nevertheless witty) entries of graffiti, newspaper headlines and bumper stickers, the Riches being the poetry, prayers and prose of fine minds that inspire by their beauty, sincerity and sublime use of words. At the lower end, I love the astringency and ability of the authors to poke fun with the sharpness of a red-hot needle. At the top end, silver words and profound wisdom sometimes lead me to tears.

All of these entries are, of course, by another hand; there is just a single entry of my own. This is plagiarism and literary theft on a considerable scale. The choice is partisan, subjective and stitched together only by the delight with which I regard them. I suppose they reflect my taste and my personality – good and bad; such a miscellany takes the risk of placing the collector on the psychiatrist's couch. Perhaps there is a certain arrogance in assembling them; after all, why should anyone else want to share my choices?

While one of the pleasures of a commonplace book is its random nature, nevertheless I have attempted to arrange these *bon mots* in some kind of order. Perhaps the travel writing entries are too numerous but I am a traveller and, for me, the descriptions are creative writing at its most lyrical and evocative. (In fact, I have shunted a few into Creativity since Travel might be overwhelmed). Poetry and Lyrics is very light on poetry; this section could have developed into an anthology all of its own but most of it would be familiar even though all of it would be exquisite. You may think that Old Age and Death occupies more than its proper share but compiling this aged seventy-five, life's departure appears rather closer than I might like, and besides, words about the conclusion of mortality have a particular poignancy and beauty. There are a number of entries from The Times since it is the paper I read and its letter page is a wonderful source of quirky British humour. You might notice that there is no section on sport, it is sparse on politics, and arid on the field of battle. Not only have I little interest in sports but I suspect that their participants have rarely time or ability to conjure up a pithy phrase; politicians sometimes have the necessary silver words but their proclamations tend to be dry and the words of military men seem confined to the pain of the war poets. Finally, on the omissions, medical entries have no chapter of their own but symptoms are scattered around the body of the text.

This is a book for the bower, the bedside, the bath and for browsing; a book at arm's length from the deck chair, for the tedium of travel but above all for pleasure. So I invite you to wallow or skip lightly. I hope there is something in this salmagundi to make you smile or catch the affections of your heart; to mingle quiet music with amiable irreverence.

Chipping Norton
April 2017

1 | The Human Condition

He wrapped himself in quotations, as a beggar would enfold himself in the purple of emperors.

Joseph Rudyard Kipling (1865-1936) Journalist, story writer, poet and novelist. Freemason. Nobel Prize for Literature. Refused Poet Laureatship and knighthood

It is not the critic who counts; not the man who points out how the strong man stumbles, or where the doer of deeds could have done them better. The credit belongs to the man who is actually in the arena, whose face is marred by dust and sweat and blood; who strives valiantly; who errs, who comes short again and again, because there is no effort without error and shortcoming; but who does actually strive to do the deeds; who knows great enthusiasms, the great devotions; who spends himself in a worthy cause; who at the best knows in the end the triumph of high achievement, and who at the worst, if he fails, at least fails while daring greatly, so that his place shall never be with those cold and timid souls who neither know victory nor defeat.

Theodore Roosevelt (1858-1919), US President (1901-1909), Paris, 23 April 1910

Sir – I am perturbed to note the number of bicycles chained to railings throughout our capital city. May I exhort the government to accede to their demands before any of them is tempted to throw itself under one of the Queen's racehorses.

Letter to The Guardian, 29 November 1992

It is difficult to love mankind unless one has a reasonable private income. And if one has a reasonable private income one has better things to do than love mankind.

Hugh Kingsmill (1889-1949), author and journalist.
Dropped Lunn from his surname

As God once said – and I think rightly...

Field Marshal Viscount Montgomery of Alamein (1887-1976).
Commander in Chief BAOR. CIGS.

Paddy Hadley, when he was Professor of Music at Cambridge, much disliked the Monday afternoon Faculty Board meetings he was required to attend. He had always lunched very well and invariably fell asleep during a lot of boring business. A succession of enraged and unsympathetic chairmen used to get him woken and try to interest the professor in their doings. 'What are the professor's views on the matter under discussion?' they would craftily ask. But Paddy was not to be put out. He had organised three answers: 'Hadley agrees with the previous speaker' he would say briskly (he usually

spoke of himself publicly in the third person), or 'Professor Hadley must confess that for the moment he is sitting on the fence'. Those were good answers, but his third was such that no chairman dared to try him again. 'Mr Chairman,' he would say, 'I have listened to the discussion with great interest but I must admit that towards the end I slightly lost the thread.

Would you be so good as to summarise the arguments to refresh me? You do these things so well.'

Glyn Daniels (1914-1986), Cambridge Professor of Archaeology (1974), from 'Some Small Harvest', 1986

Many things can be preserved in alcohol. Dignity is not one of them.

Anon

Capitalism is the exploitation of man by man. Communism is the exact reverse.

John Gardner (1926-2007), English spy and novelist

We have become, Nina, the sort of people our parents warned us about.

Augustus John (1878-1961), Welsh poet and impressionist artist, to Nina Hamnett (1890-1956), Welsh artist, known as the Queen of Bohemia

Let us now praise famous men and our fathers that begat us. The Lord hath wrought great glory by them through his great power from the beginning... Rich men furnished with ability, living peaceably in their habitations: All these were honoured in their generation and were the glory of their times.

Ecclesiasticus 44:1

On what comprises 'The Ulysses Factor: the exploring instinct in man':

Courage, practical competence, physical strength, powerful imagination, self-discipline, endurance, self-sufficiency, cunning, ability to lead, unscrupulousness and strong sexual attraction.

JRL Anderson (1911-1981), author, mountaineer and sailor, from his biography of Bill Tilman (1898-1977)

On slimming diets:

> One remedy is to eat
> lots of raw onions. These
> will not make you slim, but
> they will keep people at a distance.
> You will look slimmer at a distance.

The Independent, May 1990

Men sail a boundless and bottomless sea; there is neither harbour for shelter nor floor for anchorage, neither starting-place nor appointed destination. The enterprise is to keep afloat on an even keel; the sea is both friend and enemy; and the seamanship consists in using the resources of a traditional manner of behaviour in order to make a friend of every inimical occasion.

Michael Oakeshott (1901-1990), philosopher and political theorist

GOD GIVE US MEN!

> God give us men!
> A time like this demands strong minds,
> Great hearts, true faith and ready hands.
> Men whom the lust of office does not kill;
> Men whom the spoils of office cannot buy;
> Men who possess opinion and a will.
> Men who will not lie.

JG Holland (1819-1881), American novelist and poet

If I were asked to list values that are truly at risk, I would cite those that have no defenders and many enemies. They are so old-fashioned that they sit incongruous even on a newspaper page.

Those qualities are the triumvirate of Dignity, Courtesy and Propriety. Dignity underpins the respect we show each other, young for old, old for young and ruler for ruled. It is the 'free and equal in dignity' of the Universal Declaration of Human Rights, so rarely cited. Courtesy underpins the intercourse of reason, the conduct of debate and the tolerance of dissent. Without the rules of courtesy argument cannot progress to resolution, and art cannot flourish. Propriety lies in the honest conduct of public affairs and in what I regard as the prime duty of modern government, the uncorrupt custodianship of the built and natural environment. Without the selflessness of propriety, Britain will become a battleground of suburbs fortified against slums and swamps. Democracy will rot.

These qualities are politically neutral and infinitely fragile. They sing no tunes. No pilgrim pays them court. They are mere abstractions. Yet they form the bedrock of civilised society. As the world plunges back into the smoke of battle, I shall light them a candle and build them an altar in a corner of the gloom.

Sir Simon Jenkins (b 1943), author, editor of The Times and Evening Standard, and Chairman of the National Trust, January 2000

That woman speaks eighteen languages, and she can't say 'no' in any of them.

Dorothy Parker (1893-1867), American poet, writer and satirist. Quoted by Alexander Woolcott in his biographical essay, "Our Mrs Parker"

It was said of Sarah, Duchess of Marlborough, that she never dotted her 'i's in order to save ink.

It is only shallow people who do not judge by appearances. The mystery of the world is the visible, not the invisible.

Oscar Fingal O'Flahertie Wills Wilde (1854-1900), Irish playwright, novelist poet and wit. Gold medal for classics at Trinity, Dublin. Double first in classics at Oxford

What is wrong with being obsessed with trivia?

Barbara Pym (1913-1980), English novelist

I love children – especially when they cry, for then someone takes them away.

Nancy Mitford (1904-1973), novelist, eldest of six Mitford sisters

Happiness is having a large, caring, close-knit family in another city.

*George Burns (born Nathan Birbaum) (1896-1996),
Romanian-American comedian, actor and writer.
Still working at 100*

WC Fields, when asked whether he liked children: 'Boiled or fried?'

WC Fields (1880-1946), American comedian, actor and juggler

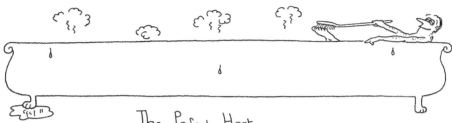

The Perfect Host

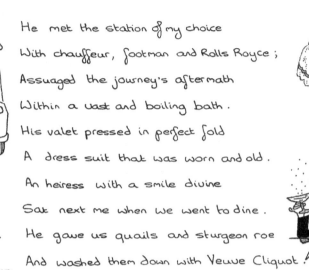

He met the station of my choice
With chauffeur, footman and Rolls Royce;
Assuaged the journey's aftermath
Within a vast and boiling bath.
His valet pressed in perfect fold
A dress suit that was worn and old.
An heiress with a smile divine
Sat next me when we went to dine.
He gave us quails and sturgeon roe
And washed them down with Veuve Cliquot.
He mounted me for every hunt,
And when my razor edge was blunt
He lent me his, and what is more
He had spare collar studs galore.
At every beat, from first to last,
His pheasants came both high and fast.
He took my I.O.U. and rent it
Said "Come again" and really meant it.

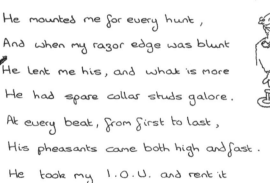

Adrian Porter

The Perfect Hostess

SHE makes you feel when you arrive
How good it is to be alive.
She promptly orders fresh-made tea
However late the hour may be.
She leads you to a comfy room
With fire ablaze — and flowers abloom.
She shows you cupboards large and wide,
No hats or frocks of <u>hers</u> inside!'
A writing-table meets your eye,
The newest novels on it lie.
The bed is just a nest of down,
Her maid puts out your dinner-gown.
The water's hot from morn till night,
Her dinners fill you with delight.
She never makes you stand for hours
Admiring children, dogs or flowers!
What better way to please her guest?
The Perfect Hostess lets you rest.

Lady Elizabeth Hester Mary von Hofmannsthal, née Paget (1916-1980),
Daughter of 6th Marquess of Anglesey

People always call me a feminist when I express opinions which differentiate me from a doormat.

Dame Rebecca West (1892-1983), author and critic

Not all creative people are notably disturbed; not all solitary people are unhappy.

Anthony Storr (1920-2001), psychiatrist

People might occasionally enjoy solitude but never loneliness; they need to feel connected and valued.

Michel de Montaigne (1533-1592), French philosopher

I enjoy solitude the way some people I know enjoy parties. It gives me an enormous sense of being alive.

Philip Roth (b 1933), American author of 'Portnoy's Complaint', 1969

Most of society's rules dictate that a man must be central, or he will sulk.

Erica Jong (b 1492), American writer, poet, feminist and author of 'Fear of Flying', 1973

The way I feel about books on sex is the way I feel about other people's holiday snaps; who wants to look at other people doing what you'd rather be doing yourself?

Anon

We act as though comfort and luxury were the chief requirements of life, when all we need to make us really happy is something to be enthusiastic about.

Charles Kingsley (1819-1875), priest, professor, historian and novelist

I can live for two months on a good compliment.

*Samuel Langhorne Clemens, known as **Mark Twain** (1835-1910),*
American humorist, entrepreneur, boat pilot, publisher

The truth is, I like it when people arrive; but I love it when they go.

***Virginia Woolf** (1882-1941), novelist, critic and depressive*

Someone who looks at me full of hope and expectation when
I come down in the morning.

***Mary Somerset**, Duchess of Beaufort (née Princess Mary of Teck)*
(1897-1987). Her definition of a nightmare guest.

The art of hospitality is to make guests feel at home when you
wish they were.

***Donald Coggan** (1909-2000), Archbishop of Canterbury*
(1974-1980)

You must come again when you have less time.

***Walter Sickert** (1860-1942), Danish-German avant-garde artist. To*
Denton Welch (1915-1948), writer and painter

Many live wires would be dead were it not for their connections.

***'Jock' Murray** (b 1938), Canadian neurologist*

We are like anyone else, only more so.

***Jean-Paul Sartre** (1905-1980), philosopher, political activist,*
playwright and novelist

There are two good reasons to buy anything: because it's very
cheap or because it's very expensive.

Anon

There are two kinds of people in this world: those who do things and those who dream of doing things.

Anon

The man who makes no mistakes does not usually make anything.

William Connor Magee (1821-1891), *Irish Archbishop of York*

My tastes are very simple. I only like the best.

Oscar Wilde (1854-1900), *Irish playwright and poet*

Sir (said he), two men of any other nation who are shown into a room together, at a house where they are both visitors, will immediately find some conversation. But two Englishmen will probably go each to a different window and remain in obstinate silence.

James Boswell (1740-1795), *Scottish lawyer and diarist.*
From 'The Life of Samuel Johnson'

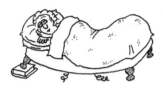

The Perfect Guest

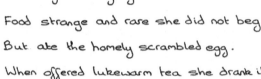

She answered by return of post
The invitation of her host.
She caught the train she said she would
And changed at junction as she should.
She brought a light and smallish box
And keys belonging to the locks.

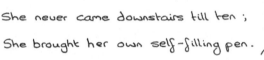

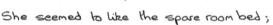

Food strange and rare she did not beg
But ate the homely scrambled egg.
When offered lukewarm tea she drank it;
She did not crave an extra blanket,
Nor extra pillows for her head!
She seemed to like the spare room bed;
She never came downstairs till ten;
She brought her own self-filling pen.
Not once by word or look of blame
Exposed her host to open shame.
She left no little things behind,
Excepting loving thoughts and kind.

*Violet Trefusis (1894-1972) writer,
socialite, lover of Vita Sackville-West.
'Trefusis never refuses'*

No Englishman can live without something to complain of.

William Hazlitt (1778-1830), critic, writer and philosopher

We should all remember that every one of us, however eminent, is a ten metre tube through which food flows, usually in one direction.

Steve Jobs (1955-2010), founder of Apple Inc, futurist and digital designer

We know little about the conscience except that it is soluble in alcohol.

Thomas Blackburn (1913-1992), American author, screenwriter and lyricist. In 'London Magazine'

Life would be dull without human error.

Anon

You can tell what God thinks of money when you look at those to whom he has given it.

Man on a train, to the publisher Colin Eccleshare

Where there's a will, there are relations.

Michael Gill (b 1960), American actor

The steel of character is forged on the anvil of adversity.

Chin-Ning Chu (b 1947), Chinese American business consultant

A free society is where it is safe to be unpopular.

Adlai Stevenson I (1835-1914), US Vice President 1893-97, Masonic Grandmaster, married Letitia Green (founder of Daughters of the American Revolution)

Men so little understand the comfort of talking a great deal about nothing at all.

Rose Leveson-Gower, Countess Granville (1890-1967), Doctor of Law

A free country is where you have the right to insult anybody.

Rowan Atkinson (b 1955), actor, comedian and screenwriter

Nothing is so annoying as to have someone go right on talking when you're interrupting!

Samuel Langhorne Clemens, known as Mark Twain (1835-1910), American writer, humorist, publisher

On the BBC Today programme, Rabbi Blue tells the story of a gay couple walking behind a girl and a boy who suddenly have a flaming row. One of the gay couple turns to the other, "That's what comes of a mixed marriage."

Lionel Blue (1930-2016) reform rabbi, broadcaster and journalist. Ex Marxist, Oxford graduate and gay

Plagiarism is quoting from one source. Research is quoting from more than one source.

Wilson Mizner (1876-1933), American raconteur, playwright and entrepreneur

If you steal from one book you are condemned as a plagiarist,
but if you steal from ten books you are considered a scholar.

Amos Oz (b 1935), Israeli writer, professor and winner of many literary prizes

If we steal our thoughts from the moderns it will be cried down
as plagiarism; if it is from the ancients it will be erudition.

*Rev Charles Caleb Colton (1781-1832), Old Etonian cleric,
writer, eccentric, art collector, gambler and author of
"Imitation is the Sincerest Form of Flattery"*

LEISURE

What is this life if, full of care,
We have no time to stand and stare.

No time to stand beneath the boughs
And stare as long as sheep and cows.

No time to see when woods we pass
Where squirrels hide their nuts in grass.

No time to see, in broad daylight,
Streams full of stars, like skies at night.

No time to turn at Beauty's glance,
And watch her feet, how they can dance.

No time to wait till her mouth can
Enrich that smile her eyes began.

A poor life this if, full of care,
We have no time to stand and stare.

*William Davies (1871-1940), Welsh poet who spent
much of his life in America living as a hobo*

The Copy Cat

The perfect guest, the perfect pest,
We have discussed each case with zest
Determined to give tit-for-tat.
But now... About the Copy Cat.

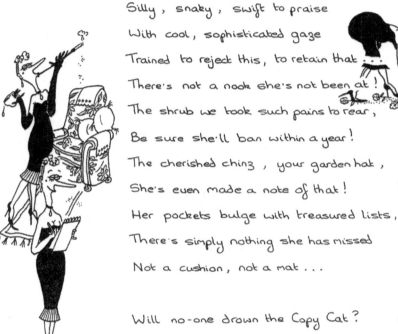

Silly, snaky, swift to praise
With cool, sophisticated gaze
Trained to reject this, to retain that
There's not a nook she's not been at!
The shrub we took such pains to rear,
Be sure she'll ban within a year!
The cherished chinz, your garden hat,
She's even made a note of that!
Her pockets bulge with treasured lists,
There's simply nothing she has missed
Not a cushion, not a mat...

Will no-one drown the Copy Cat?

Anon

He kept an open mind so long
That everything fell out
And false and true
And right and wrong
Were scrambled into doubt.

Quoted by Frances Hoare (née Hogg)

Ill fares the land, to hastening ills a prey,
Where wealth accumulates and men decay.

Oliver Goldsmith (1730-1774), Irish novelist, poet and friend
of Samuel Johnson, from 'The Deserted Village'

But how much more unfortunate are those
Where wealth decays and population grows.

Hilaire Belloc (1870-1953), Anglo-French writer,
poet and member of parliament

Success is the necessary misfortune of human life, but it is only
to the very unfortunate that it comes early.

Anthony Trollope (1815-1882), novelist

If you can keep your head while those about you are losing
theirs, perhaps you do not understand the situation.

Nelson Boswell (d. 2002), American author and college professor,
from 'Successful Living Day by Day', 1972

The one important thing I have learnt over the years is the
difference between taking one's work seriously and taking
oneself seriously. The first is imperative – the second disastrous.

Dame Margot Fonteyn de Arias (1919-1991), Prima Ballerina Assoluta

The most valuable thing I have learned from life is to regret nothing. Life is short, nature is hostile and man is ridiculous. But oddly enough, most misfortunes have their compensations, and with a certain humour and a great deal of horse sense, we can make a fairly good job of what is, after all, a matter of very small consequence.

Somerset Maugham (1874-1965), naturalist, playwright and
intelligence officer

Happiness is nothing more than good health and a bad memory.

Dr Albert Schweitzer (1875-1965), German-French medical
missionary, music scholar and philosopher

A good conversationalist is, first and foremost, a good listener. In fact, among people who are widely regarded as great conversationalists, there are some who hardly ever open their mouths at all.

Quentin Crisp (born Denis Charles Pratt) (1908-1999), effeminate writer
and actor. From 'Doing it in Style', 1981

To own a bit of ground, to scratch it with a hoe, to plant seeds, and watch their renewal of life – this is the commonest delight of the race, the most satisfactory thing a man can do.

Charles Dudley
Warner (1829-1900),
American novelist and
friend of Mark Twain

A pompous woman of his acquaintance, complaining that the head-waiter of a restaurant had not shown her and her husband immediately to a table, said, 'We had to tell him who we were.' Gerald, interested, enquired, 'And who were you?'

Gerald Tyrwhitt-Wilson, 14th Baron Berners (1887-1964), composer, painter, novelist and aesthete, about Dame Edith Sitwell, eccentric poet and sister of Osbert and Sacheverell

THE GOLDEN JOURNEY TO SAMARKAND

We travel not for trafficking alone;
By hotter winds our fiery hearts are fanned;
For lust of knowing what should not be known,
We take the Golden Road to Samarkand

We are the pilgrims, Master; we shall go
Always a little further; it may be
Beyond that last blue mountain barred with snow
Across that angry or that glimmering sea.

James Elroy Flecker (1884-1915), poet, novelist and playwright. Started as a diplomat in the Middle East before his death aged 30. The last verse is inscribed on the clock tower of the SAS regimental headquarters in Hereford

The mind makes appointments the body cannot keep.

John Arlott (1914-1991), journalist, author and cricket commentator

I've learnt so much from my mistakes, I'm thinking of making a few more.

*Clifford Price, known as **Goldie** (b 1965), electronic music artist, disc jockey, actor, graffiti artist*

When asked by a visiting journalist how many worked in the Vatican, Pope John thought for a while and replied, "About half."

Pope John Paul II, born Karol Jozef Wojtyla (1920-2005), canonised April 2014

Women get lost, men take an unscheduled alternative route.

Nick Harding (b 1964), screen writer, journalist and author

AN ALTERNATIVE TO SHAKESPEAR'S SEVEN AGES OF MAN

First puking and mewling,
Then pissed off with schooling,
Then f***ing and fights,
Then judging chap's rights,
Then sitting in slippers and ending up drooling.

Robert Conquest (1917-2015), diplomat, soviet expert, womaniser and part time poet

America is the only country in the world that has gone from barbarism to decadence without an intervening period of civilization.

Georges Clemenceau (1841-1929), French Prime Minister during WWI. Married Mary Plummer from New York

This is the true joy of life... the being a force of Nature instead of a feverish little clod of ailments and grievances complaining that the world will not devote itself to making you happy.

George Bernard Shaw (1856-1950), Irish playwright and critic. From the preface to 'Man and Superman', 1903

To be in love with oneself is the beginning of a lifelong romance' and to this I add: and in every way most satisfactory, and safe.

AL Rowse (1903-1997), historian of Elizabethan England.
From 'Portrait and Views', 1986

Non est vivere, sed valere, vita est.
[Life is not only being alive, but being well.]

Sulla (d. 78BC), Roman general and statesman

In the Memorial Park of Alert Bay (an island in spite of its name) off Vancouver Island, there is a tablet whose carved inscription recognises the contribution of Gilbert Popovich, an ex-mayor. It ends 'He lived with grace' and a wag has added 'but died with Gretel'.

In human relations kindness and lies are worth a thousand truths.

Graham Greene (1904-1991), English novelist, traveller and spy.
Estranged from wife and children

Things cannot go on getting worse, one thinks, and then they do get worse.

John Stewart Collis (1900-1984), Irish biographer

'She never loved him [Sebastian], you know, as we do.' 'Do.'
The word reproached me; there was no past tense in Cordelia's verb 'to love'.

Evelyn Waugh (1903-1966), novelist, biographer and travel writer.
From 'Brideshead Revisited', 1945

Money talks, wealth whispers.

Attributed to **Warren Buffet** *(b 1930), investor and philanthropist,*
known as 'The Wizard of Omaha'

That money talks I'll not deny,
I heard it once, it said 'Goodbye'

Richard Armour *(1906-1989), American poet*

Tyrants appear great only because we are on our knees.

Etienne de la Boetie *(1530-1563), French judge, philosopher,*
essayist and poet

One must, it is true, forgive one's enemies; but not before they
are hanged.

Heinrich Heine *(1797-1856), German journalist, literary critic*
and poet. His poetry is set to music by Schubert and Schumann

There are two things that people will always pay for – food
and sex. I am no good at cooking.

Fernande Grudet, aka **Madame Claude,** *(1923-2015), French*
procurer to the rich and famous from a brothel above Rothschild's
bank in Paris. Innovator of the 'call girl' – to book by telephone

When choosing between two evils, I always like to try the one
I've never tried before.

Mary Jane 'Mae' West (1893-1980), American actress, singer,
playwright, comedienne and sex symbol

Everyone has talent. The difficulty is having it at 50.

*Hilaire-Germain-**Edgar Degas** (formerly de Gas) (1834-1917), French painter and sculptor. Creole mother from New Orleans, father a banker*

The best qualification for a prophet is to have a good memory.

Edward Lindley Wood, 1st Earl of Halifax (1881-1959), Viceroy of India, Foreign Secretary, Ambassador to Washington, Fellow of All Souls, Master of Middleton foxhounds, Chancellor of Oxford University. Born with no left hand

Would you like to sin
With Elinor Glyn
On a tiger skin?
Or would you prefer
To err with her
On some other fur?

Anon. *Elinor Glyn (1864-1943), writer of racy novels. Born Jersey, Channel Islands*

She left as she arrived. Fired with enthusiasm.

Reference for a departing housemaid

She was a good cook and as good cooks go, she went.

*HH Munro (known as **Saki**) (1870-1916), gay writer and satirist. Born in Burma. Killed in battle*

Early to rise and early to bed
Makes a man healthy and socially dead

Charles Baker Creswell (b 1935)

'*Early to bed and early to rise*' is a desirable attribute in many conscientious workers. So thought a Danish company that recommended this in a staff memo – '*Hurtig i seng og op med hanen*'. Its UK office translated this as '*Quick into bed and up with the cock*'.

Among correspondence on what makes a gentleman, was the assertion that no gentleman would play the accordion. This prompted the following letter:

> Sir, An accordionist once left his accordion on the back seat of his locked car. He returned to find the rear window smashed and three more accordions added.
>
> **Iain Macniven,** November 2016

You know when there is a secret for it is whispered around everywhere.

> **William Congreve** *(1670-1729), dramatist and poet.*
> *From Love for Love 1605*

It was well known that Helen Gurney Brown had many visits to cosmetic surgeons. The opening paragraph of her obituary in the New York Times was accurate but rather bitchy: 'She was ninety, although parts of her were considerably younger'.

> **Helen Gurley Brown** *(1922-2012), American author, business woman and philanthropist. Editor of Cosmopolitan 1965-1997*

If you want peace, don't talk to your friends. Talk to your enemies.

> **Desmond Tutu** *(b 1931), South African social rights activist and Anglican Archbishop. Nobel Peace Prize, Albert Schweitzer Prize, Pacem in Terris Award, Sydney Peace Prize, Gandhi Peace Prize, and Presidential Medal of Freedom. Fist Class Degree in Theology from Kings College, London*

Marriage: just because you are on a diet there is no reason why you shouldn't look at the menu.

Marriage: on with the shackles – out with the shekels.

Marriage: a chain so heavy that it always takes two people to carry it – sometimes three.

Where there are no arguments or fights it is a dead marriage.

Anon

Marriage is a dangerous relationship, full of potential destruction of personality. People aren't meant to be together twenty-four hours a day.

Dame Margaret Drabble, Lady Holroyd (b 1939),
novelist and biographer

Love is blind but marriage restores the sight.

Georg Christoph Lichtenberg (1742 – 1799), German scientist,
satirist, and Anglophile

He has the body of a twenty-five-year-old.

Margaret Trudeau (1919-2000), of her husband, Pierre,
Prime Minister of Canada

When the Sultan arrived home early, his wife let out a terrified sheikh!

Christmas cracker

One cannibal to another: 'I don't like your mother-in-law.'
'Well – just eat the vegetables!'

Christmas cracker

No son-in-law was ever good enough for his mother-in-law.

Anon

Say it in diamonds, say it in mink,
Whatever you do, don't say it in ink.

Julius Henry 'Groucho' Marx (1890 1977), comedian,
film and television star. 26 movies.

Don't question your wife's judgement – look whom she married!

Anon

And in the end the only thing worth having is laughter and the love of friends.

GK Chesterton (1874-1936), poet, theologian, philosopher,
literary critic, dramatist and biographer

There is, of course, no reason for the existence of the male sex, except that one sometimes needs help in moving the piano.
Dame Rebecca West (1892-1983), *author, journalist, travel writer and feminist*

Contraceptives: used by Protestants on all conceivable occasions.

Terence **'Spike' Milligan** *(1918-2002), comedian, writer and actor. Son of Captain Alphonso Milligan. Educated at St Paul's, Rangoon*

Love is not looking in each other's eyes, but looking together in the same direction.

Antoine de Saint-Exupéry (1900-1944), *French aristocrat, author and aviator*

A first-class wife and a second-class brain will defeat first-class brains and a second-class wife.

Anon

… nothing in this world was more difficult than love.

Gabriel García Márquez *(known as Gabito throughout Latin America) (1927-2014), socialist Colombian novelist, screenwriter and journalist*

There is no reciprocity. Men love women, women love children, children love hamsters.

Alice Thomas Ellis (1932-2005), part Finnish, part Welsh,
sometime nun and novelist

Mere passion is only the beginning of love. People who don't have children and don't go through troubles together can't really love. So they move like bees from one appetite to another.

Malcolm Muggeridge (1903-1990), journalist, author, satirist,
religious and moral campaigner

In an ideal relationship, both partners know they can live perfectly well without each other, but they also know they much prefer to live with each other.

Karen Horney (1885-1952), German psychoanalyst and
opponent of Freudian views

FAMILY AND STATE

Throughout the ages, political philosophers, social historians, and civic and religious leaders have praised the family as the foundation of social order, the bedrock of nations and the bastion of civilisation. The family is a universal and irreplaceable community, rooted in human nature and the basis for all societies at all times. As the cradle of life and love for each new generation, the family is the primary source of personal identity, self-esteem, and support for children. It is also the first and foremost school of life, uniquely suited to teach children integrity, character, morals, responsibility, service and wisdom.

Dr Wade F Horn, psychologist, US Department of Health, 2001

Behind every successful man stands a surprised woman.

Maryon Pearson (1901-1989), wife of Canadian Prime Minister
Lester Pearson (1897-1972)

The UN Declaration of Human Rights describes the family as 'The natural and fundamental group unit of society.'

MAKE LOVE NOT WAR.
AMO, AMAS, AMAT IT AGAIN

Victoria Station

In 1947 John Wyndham took his young wife to Petworth to meet his Uncle Charles, the frosty, feudal 3rd Lord Leconfield. 'Looking out of the White Library window on a beautiful summer's day over the Capability Brown park with the stretch of water about the size of the Serpentine in the foreground, she said, wishing to please as well as being entranced by the view, 'Oh, Cousin Charles, what a beautiful lake!' There followed a thunder-laden silence, broken by Uncle Charles saying in the most magisterial tone: 'My dear young lady, one day your husband will inherit from me not only all this, but also among other things in Cumberland, half Derwentwater, the whole of Bassenthwaite Lake and the whole of Wastwater, comprising in all about 35 square miles of lake. That which you see there is not a lake. It is a pond.

Part of the obituary of Pamela, Dowager Lady Egremont, The Times,
10 October 2014

Most virtuous women, like hidden treasures, are secure because nobody seeks after them.

François de la Rochefoucauld (1613-1680),
French nobleman and writer, from 'Maxims'

It is difficult to define love. But we may say that in the soul, it is a ruling passion; in the mind, it is a close sympathy and affinity; in the body, a wholly secret and delicate longing to possess what we love – and this is after much mystery.

Ibid

I've thought of you all my life. Even before I met you, I thought of you as the promise to come.

John Grisham (b 1955), American lawyer, politician
and author. From 'The Firm', 1991

THE PASSIONATE SHEPHERD TO HIS LOVE

Come live with me and be my Love,
And we will all the pleasures prove
That hills and valleys, dale and field,
And all the craggy mountains yield.

There will we sit upon the rocks
And see the shepherds feed their flocks,
By shallow rivers, to whose falls
Melodious birds sing madrigals.

There will I make thee beds of roses
And a thousand fragrant posies,
A cap of flowers, and a kirtle
Embroider'd all with leaves of myrtle.

A gown made of the finest wool
Which from our pretty lambs we pull,
Fair linèd slippers for the cold,
With buckles of the purest gold.

A belt of straw and ivy buds
With coral clasps and amber studs:
And if these pleasures may thee move,
Come live with me and be my Love.

Thy silver dishes for thy meat
As precious as the gods do eat,
Shall on an ivory table be
Prepared each day for thee and me.

The shepherd swains shall dance and sing
For they delight each May-morning:
If these delights thy mind may move,
Then live with me and be my Love.

Christopher Marlowe (1564(?)-1593), Elizabethan poet and playwright

Don't walk in front, I may not follow;
Don't walk behind, I may not lead;
But walk beside me and be my friend.

Albert Camus (1913-1960), French Nobel Prize winning
author, communist, philosopher and founder of Absurdism

Constant use has not worn ragged the fabric of friendship.

Dorothy Parker (1863-1967), American poet, critic and satirist

To see the world in a grain of sand and heaven in a wild flower,
Hold infinity in the palms of your hands and eternity in an hour.

William Blake (1757-1827), poet and printer

WHEN YOU ARE OLD

When you are old and grey and full of sleep,
And nodding by the fire, take down this book,
And slowly read, and dream of the soft look
Your eyes had once, and of their shadows deep;

How many loved moments of glad grace
And loved your beauty with love false or true,
But one man loved the pilgrim soul in you,
And loved the sorrows of your changing face;

And bending down beside the glowing bars,
Murmur, a little sadly, how love fled
And paced upon the mountain overhead
And hid his face amid a crowd of stars.

William Butler Yeats (1865-1939), Irish poet, Nationalist
and Senator, Nobel Prize in Literature

Wine comes in at the mouth
And love comes in at the eye;
That's all we know for truth
Before we grow old and die.
I lift the glass to my mouth,
I look at you, and I sigh.

Ibid

DAYBREAK

At dawn she lay with her profile at that angle
Which, when she sleeps, seems the carved face of an angel.
Her hair a harp, the hand of breeze follows
And plays, against the white cloud of the pillows.
Then, in a flush of rose, she woke and her eyes that opened
Swam in blue through her rose flesh that dawned.
From the dew of lips, the drop of one word
Fell like the first of fountains; murmured
'Darling'. Upon my ears the song of the first bird.
'My dream becomes my dream,' she said, 'come true.
I waken from you to my dream of you.'
Oh, my own wakened dream than dared assume
The audacity of her sleep. Our dreams
Poured into each other's arms, like streams.

*Sir Stephen Spender (1909-1995), poet, novelist and essayist,
Poet Laureate to US Library of Congress, Emeritus Professor of
English at University College, London. Gay but married.
Daughter married Australian comedian Barry Humphries*

THE GOURMET'S LOVE-SONG

How strange is love; I am not one
Who Cupid's power belittles,
For Cupid 'tis who make me shun
My customary victuals.
Oh, Effie, since that painful scene
That left me broken-hearted,
My appetite, erstwhile so keen,
Has utterly departed.

My form, my friends observe with pain,
Is growing daily thinner.
Love only occupies the brain
That once would think of dinner.
Around me myriad waiters flit,
With meat and drink to ply men;
Alone, disconsolate, I sit,
And feed on thoughts of Hymen.

The kindly waiters hear my groan,
They strive to charm with curry;
They tempt me with a devilled bone –
I beg them not to worry.
Soup, whitebait, entrées, fricassées,
They bring me uninvited.
I need them not, for what are these
To one whose life is blighted?

*Sir Pelham Grenville Wodehouse (**PG Wodehouse**, known as Plum)*
(1881-1975), humorist author, playwright and controversial broadcaster

KISSES IN THE TRAIN

I saw the Midlands
Revolve through her hair;
The fields of Autumn
Stretching bare,
And sheep on the pasture
Tossed back in a stare.
And still as ever
The world went round,
My mouth was on her pulsing
Neck was found,
And my breast to her beating
Breast was bound.

And the world was all whirling
Around in joy
Like the dance of a dervish
Did destroy
My sense and my reason
spun like a toy.

*DH Lawrence (1885-1930), novelist, poet, playwright, essayist, literary
critic, painter and traveller*

A man who can drive safely while kissing a girl
is simply not giving the kiss enough attention.

3 | Travel

OZMANDIAS OF EGYPT

I met a traveller from an antique land
Who said: Two vast and trunkless legs of stone
Stand in the desert. Near them on the sand,
Half sunk, a shatter'd visage lies, whose frown
And wrinkled lip and sneer of cold command
Tell that its sculptor well those passions read
Which yet survive, stamp'd on these lifeless things,
The hand that mock'd them and the heart that fed;
And on the pedestal these words appear:
'My name is Ozymandias, king of kings:
Look on my works, ye Mighty, and despair!'
Nothing beside remains. Round the decay
Of that colossal wreck, boundless and bare,
The lone and level sands stretch far away.

*Percy Bysshe Shelley (1792-1822), romantic poet. The fictional
Ozymandias was inspired by an enormous fallen head that
lies on the bank of the Nile.*

In thought faith
In word wisdom
In deed courage
In life service.
– So may India be great.

*Inscription on the base of the Jaipur Column which stands before the
main front of Viceroy's House, New Delhi*

There is no such thing as bad weather, only unsuitable clothing.

Alfred Wainwright (1907-1991), fellwalker,
guidebook author and illustrator

What a bore it is to go out when one would much rather stay home.

Marcel Proust, (1871-1922), author of
'A la recherche du temps perdu', 1913-1927

The world is a book and those who do not travel read only one page.

St Augustine (354-430)

The preferred form of travel of *Gustave Flaubert (1821-1880)* was to lie on a divan and have the scenery carried past him.

The best thing about travel is that it teaches what are the places that are not worth seeing.

Pierre Bénoit (1886-1962), French novelist

... I had time to have a quiet beer with an old friend and a plate of chicken satay in one of those back lanes that made Gide call the city 'Kuala l'impure'.

Paul Theroux (b 1941), American novelist and travel writer, from 'The Great Railway Bazaar', 1975

As the days passed I slowed down and, with Nagel's Turkey in my hand, began sightseeing, an activity that delights the truly idle because it seems so much like scholarship, gawping and eavesdropping on antiquity, flattering oneself with the notion that one is discovering the past when really one is inventing it, using a guidebook as a scenario of swift notations.

Ibid.

Nowhere can you find a combination more breathtaking of sea and snow, age and vigour, history and persiflage. Only at the Levantine end of the Mediterranean could a Beirut exist, with all its undertones of antiquity, graft and tolerance. Is she really a great city, this wayward paragon? Scarcely by the standards of Berlin or San Francisco, Tokyo or Moscow; but she is great in a different kind. She is great like a voluptuous courtesan, a shady merchant prince, the scent of jasmine or the flash of a dazzling scandal. She has scarcely achieved greatness, nor even had it thrust upon her: but greatness has often spent a night in her arms, and a little lingers.

James Morris (b 1926), 9th Queen's Lancers, and Times correspondent at the ascent of Everest (1953). Father of five children, transitioned to living as a female (1972). From 'Cities' (written before the destruction of 1976-1985)

All the Middle East makes for Beirut. Here you may see the political exiles, talking dark and interminable subterfuge, or the resplendent hawk-nosed sheikhs, in all the gilded refulgence of the Arab patrimony, fingering their beads and indulging in flamboyant bickering. Here are the silken ladies of Syria, svelte and doe-eyed, and here are the waterside harlots, curled but smouldering, Semite with a touch of baroque. There are many poets in Beirut, and artists of visionary tendencies, shaggy existentialists in frayed sandals, dilettantes by the score, spies by the portfolio. Sometimes you may see Druse tribesmen in the city, out of the eastern hills, ferociously hirsute and gloriously swaggering. Sometimes the fleet puts in (British, American, French or Greek) and the waterfront bars are loud with ribaldry. And when one of the perennial Middle Eastern Crises erupts into the headlines, then the imperturbable hotels of Beirut are crammed again with foreign correspondents, the hall porters brush up their jargon and sniff around for tittle-tattle, and the whole city seems transformed into one sensitive, quivering antenna.

But in Beirut you are seldom in the heart of things. The firemen are always visiting, the crisis is usually somewhere else. It feels a transitory place, like an exceedingly corrupt and sophisticated girls' school. Such a way of life, you feel, cannot be permanent: it is all too fickle, too fast, too make-believe and never-never. It is Alexandria without the philosophers, without the Pharaohs, perhaps even without Cleopatra (for age does distinctly wither the grandes dames of Beirut, waddling with poodles and sunglasses from salon to couturier). For all its age and history Beirut feels a rootless city – salacious but not earthy, virile but infertile. A breath of wind, it seems, a shift of fortune, and all this bright-painted fabric would be whisked away into oblivion.

James Morris, on 1950s Beirut, from 'A Writer's World', 2003

There are still, I found, no mornings like French town mornings, when the bread hangs fragrant upon the awakening air, when the priests converge blackly upon the cathedral for early mass, and the whine of the mopeds about the Place de la Gare incites the first tourist to throw open her shutters and sip her orange juice in the sunshine.

... I went to one such restaurant, on such an apathetic Sunday, in one of those ancient towns of central France where the streets wind upwards from the railway track, through scowling walls of medievalism, until they debouch in the square outside the cathedral door, surveyed by huge stone animals through the stone latticework of the cathedral tower, and prowled about on Sunday mornings by cats and desultory visitors... It remained quintessential France, as we islanders have loved and loathed it for several centuries. Madame remained the epitome of everything false, narrow-minded and

unreliable. One waiter seemed, as ever, to be some sort of a duke, the other was evidently the village idiot. At the table next to mine sat a prosperous local family out for Sunday dinner, well known to the proprietress and esteemed throughout the community – unsmiling, voluminously napkinned, serious and consistent eaters who sometimes, eyeing me out of the corners of their piggy eyes, exchanged in undertones what were doubtless scurrilous sly Anglophobics, before returning sluggishly to their veal.

James Morris, on France in the 1990s, also from 'A Writer's World'

Sometimes a gaunt horse hauls a sledge lop-sidedly down a road, piled high with baskets and packing-cases; or a car ploughs past with a puff of oily exhaust and a whiff of crude oil; or a great rough-hewn lorry, painted a sombre green and wrapped around the bonnet with quilted fabric, rumbles darkly through the trees; and presently there appear through the misted windscreen the first tokens of the city. A suburban trolley-bus slides alongside, painted a bright blue and yellow, its windows so steamy that only a blur of head-scarves and wrinkled faces can dimly be seen, or the pink tip of a child's nose pressed against the glass. The traffic thickens, the empty countryside falls away, and soon there looms out of the fitful snowfall a monstrous parade of buildings. Huge, square and forbidding they appear, of no definable style or period, like so many vast eight-storey breeding-houses. They look shuttered and deserted, but for a bleak light here and there, and they rise sheer and stern on each side of the road, window after window, block after block, mile after mile, like enormous piles of ammunition boxes in some remote and secret dump. Only a few squat women move in and out of their vault-like doors, and the television aerials standing awry on their roofs seem sad but lovable impertinences. Immensely wide is the street that strikes through this gloomy cavalcade, and presently the rhythm of the buildings shifts, like a train crossing the points. Dreadful symmetry gives way to a jumble of old and new and indeterminate: a sagging, classical portico behind high walls, a rickety cul-de-sac of single-storey chalets, the plaster and lath peeling to show the criss-cross beneath; a bridge across a frozen river, its ornamental urns stacked with sculptured rifles, swords, trumpets and machine guns. The traveller rubs his window with his fur hat, and sees that the city has closed in upon him.

James Morris, on entering Moscow in Winter. Written soon after the death of Joseph Stalin in 1953. Another from 'A Writer's World'

The heaviest baggage is an empty purse.

German proverb

As a member of an escorted group, you don't even have to know that the Matterhorn isn't a tuba.

Fielding's Travel Guide to Europe, 1963

Checking into my hotel in the Rue de Seine, on the Left Bank between Boulevard Saint Germain and the river, it occurred to me that I had moved up in the world. There was a pillow. Whenever I was in Paris during the Sixties – and it was never often enough, alas – I could afford only the kind of hotel where they gave you what felt like a rolling-pin wrapped in calico. You could bash yourself over the head with this in hopes of rendering yourself dizzy enough to get some sleep on a bed that resembled a ping-pong table without the flexibility. There used to be a jug of cold water standing in a bowl. You poured the water into the bowl, spread some of it upon your person, dried yourself with a towel which had previously seen service as a bandage during the days of the Commune, and pronounced yourself clean.

Clive James (b 1939), Australian poet, broadcaster, writer and critic.
From 'Flying Visits', 1984

I did not understand the term 'terminal illness' until I saw Heathrow.

Dennis Potter (1935-1994), dramatist, screen writer, journalist
and Russian speaker

We came down, as a ghost sinks through a wall, beneath a canopy of sculpted cloud, and circled the magnificent cradle of mountains surrounding the Shomali plain in the absinthine light of the setting sun. It flashed as we spiralled downward, first over the right wing and then the left, like a luminous and gigantesque gold coin. From it a final volley of long light-filled lances flew earthwards between the crenellations of the upper ridges, and under their gilded trajectory, clusters of tiny settlements glinted from the snowbound fields below like the illuminated letters of a parchment.

Just then, somewhere far away to the west, the clouds broke and released a burst of afternoon sunlight that fell in a luminous swathe across the valley. Quite suddenly the minarets were transformed and danced unexpectedly to life, no longer the forlorn colour of mud but a regal shade of turquoise, shimmering with golden highlights against the curtain of dark cloud behind them. It lasted only a moment but my sense of grief was suddenly lifted, as if a whisper, husky with the intimacy of the past, had stolen furtively across the centuries as a reminder that, despite everything, time's respect for beauty was not entirely undone.

Jason Elliot (b 1965), travel writer, on flying into Herat, from
'An Unexpected Light: Travels in Afghanistan', 2007

They were delightfully, seedily British, almost of an earlier, harder, less neurotic age. From their bad teeth and unhealthy complexions to their coarse, deadpan humour, from Frank's baggy, wide-stitched cardigans and old stained grey trousers to Keith's dark blue pea-jacket and old-fashioned sailor's blue cap, they called to mind stories by WW Jacobs of foggy ports and erring captains' daughters, and lines by Masefield on tramps in dirty Channel weather carrying cargoes of ironware and cheap tin trays. They brought back to me an early twentieth-century world in which sailors still carried ditty-boxes and parrots in cages; a world of greasy mess room plates, the cook's thumbprint in the gravy, piled with fatty pork and waterlogged spuds and peas that had first been dried like dead men's eyes and then drowned like unwanted puppies; of thick chunks of bread called 'doorsteps' smeared with beef dripping; of suet pudding called 'spotted dog' you could have thrown overboard and anchored a Swansea collier to. A dingier world, maybe, but not one that, compared to today need feel ashamed of itself. This was the way to come back to Blighty. Not on some spick-and-span, soulless, automatic container ship.

Gavin Young (1928-2001), travel writer, from 'Slow Boats Home', 1981

Noel Coward was an inveterate sender of telegrams.

To his companion, Cole Lesley, he wired:
'am back from istanbul where i was known as english delight.'

When he was staying in Florence, he cabled home:
'have moved hotel excelsior. coughing myself into a firenze.'

Sir Noel Coward (1899-1973), playwright, composer, director,
singer, lyricist

To move, to breathe, to fly, to float
To gain all while you give
To roam the roads of lands remote,
To travel is to live

Hans Christian Andersen (1805-1875), Danish playwright,
novelist, poet and writer of fairy tales

These following quotations were first gathered together with chapter headings for my book 'The Last Blue Mountain'.

But why, oh why do the wrong people travel when the right people stay at home?

Noel Coward

Life for him was an adventure; perilous indeed, but men are not made for safe havens.

Edith Hamilton on Aeschylus

I have just been round the world and formed a very poor opinion of it.

Sir Thomas Beecham

The only way of catching a train I ever discovered was to miss the train before.

GK Chesterton

I have found that there ain't no surer way to find out whether you like people or hate them, than to travel with them.

Mark Twain

Not all those who wander are lost.

JRR Tolkien

Stop worrying about the potholes and celebrate the journey.

Fitzhugh Mullan

Do not follow where the path may lead. Go instead where there is no path and leave a trail.

Ralph Waldo Emerson

I have not been everywhere but it's on my list.

Susan Sontag

Tourists wander for distraction, travellers ramble for fulfilment.

Hilaire Belloc

My favourite thing is to go where I have never gone.

Diane Arbus

No vacation goes unpunished.

Karl Hakkarainen

The world is getting such a dangerous place one is lucky to get out of it alive.

WC Fields

For the born traveller, travelling is a besetting vice. Like other vices, it is imperious, demanding of the victim's time, money and energy and the sacrifice of comfort.

Aldous Huxley

If you come to a fork in the road, take it.

Yogi Berra

One always begins to forgive a place as soon as it is left behind.

Charles Dickens

A man of superior talents (which I cannot deny myself to be without being impious) will go to pieces if he remains forever in the same place.

Wolfgang Amadeus Mozart

Leave the home, O youth, and seek out alien shores.

Petronius

Mountains are not chivalrous. Indifferently, they lash those who venture among them with snow, rock, wind and cold.

George Schaller

The normal stigmata of a travel book are the fake intensities, discovering the 'soul' of a town after spending two hours in it and the boring descriptions of conversations with taxi drivers.

George Orwell

I have seldom heard a train go by and not wished I was on it.

Paul Theroux

For day wear, drill or palm beach shirts are general. Revolvers are not usually necessary.

South American Handbook, 1947

The monsoon is India's sensuous season. After months of stifling heat, the rains refresh not only the arid land but man's parched spirit. The slow, rhythmic slap of the tabla drum and the languorous whine of the eight-string sitar echo in the rain-splashed night. Painters show lovers on a balcony gazing out over the greening landscape as a peacock, its rainbow tail spread wide, struts its monsoon dance. Poets celebrate the mythical chataka bird which lives on raindrops or they sing of monsoon love... But here on the dun plains of the Ganges basin the monsoon of song and painting is only a gauzy memory. No peacocks or raindrop-eating chataka birds here – only the brown sparrow grubbing for dead seeds in the furrow. No lovers on a balcony – only villagers breaking stones in the forest to earn a handful of grain. No tabla and no sitar – just the plaintive bleat of the Brahman's conch horn asking the gods for rain.

J Anthony Lukas (1933-1997), Pulitzer Prize winner, journalist and author.
From 'Village of Hunger and Lethargy', 1976

With smoke and sparks streaming from is bulbous funnel, here it comes at ten miles an hour along the wide straight road. On the driving platform of its three-wheeled traction engine, surrounded mysteriously by wheels, valves and levers, sit the European engineer and his assistant, one in a toupee, one in a soft black cap, with bright kerchiefs around their necks, and expressions of resolute professionalism. There is a cyclopean light on the front of the engine, and its wheels are vast, solid and clad in rubber. Majestically clanking and puffing it approaches us, and now we see the turbanned Sikh fireman sitting with his piles of logs in the tender, and behind him the long line of the train – two-wheeled carts alternating with high four-wheeled wagons, like English hay-wains, and far at the back, wobbling slightly on its passage and raising a cloud of dust, a closed passenger carriage thickly covered, inside and out, with white robed travellers – standing on the couplings, hanging to the doors, crouched precarious upon the roof.

The great machine passes us. The engineer courteously removes his hat. The fireman grins, bows repeatedly and murmurs inaudible respects. The carts and wagons rumble by. The crowded passengers at the back stare down at us expressionless but superior, as though they have been admitted to some higher existence. With a stately hoot of its steam-whistle the Government Steam Train, unquestionably steering a way to Glory, ponderously but imperially disappears.

Paul Theroux (b 1941), American novelist and travel writer.
From 'The Great Railway Bazaar', 1975

Of all the world's countries, India is the most truly prodigious, and this quality of astonishment displays itself afresh every day as the sun comes up in Delhi. Five hundred and eighty million people, 300 languages, provinces from the Himalayan to the equatorial, cities as vast as Bombay and Calcutta,

It wasn't half bad. But this was only because I left at the interval.

Baron Finkelstein (b 1962), journalist and politician.
On a play, quoted in The Times

The difference... between the person who says he 'wishes to be a writer' and the person who says he 'wishes to write'. The former desires to be pointed out at cocktail parties, the latter is prepared for the long, solitary hours at a desk; the former desires a status; the latter a process; the former desires to be, the latter to do.

Sir John Mortimer (1923-2009), barrister, author and dramatist

... note it in a book, that it may be for the time to come for ever and ever.

Isaiah 30:8

Contrary to popular impression, writers, unlike pole vaulters, do not know when they have done their best...

John Updike (1932-2009), American author, critic and poet

Fall asleep reading a good book and you enter a world of dreams; fall asleep in a film and you miss the end.

Stephen Amidon (b 19690), American author and film critic

We have read your manuscript with boundless delight. If we were to publish your paper, it would be impossible for us to publish any work of a lower standard. And as it is unthinkable that in the next thousand years we shall see its equal we are to our regret compelled to return your divine composition and beg you a thousand times to overlook our short sight and timidity.

Chinese rejection slip

Publisher to author: 'It is a remarkable write, but not an irresistible read.'

Cartoon in The New Yorker

It is unwise ever to give a publisher an outline... it is like playing the proposed themes of a symphony with one finger.

Anthony Burgess (born John Anthony Burgess Wilson) (1917-1933), comic writer (known for 'A Clockwork Orange') and composer of 250 musical works

I have to drive myself into the nasty bits of writing. It's like climbing a steep hill, forcing your legs all the way. It can be extraordinarily unpleasant. Though the view can be wonderful.

Dame Margaret Drabble / Lady Holroyd (1939-2014), prolific novelist and academic, mother of gardener Joe Swift and sister of AS Byatt. Starred First at Oxford for literature

... you will find that people who lack elementary culture keep books not as tools of learning but as a decoration for their dining-rooms. So we should buy enough books for use, and none just for embellishment.

Seneca (4BC–65AD), philosopher and Roman statesman

If your writing isn't working, the reader will go into the kitchen and make a cheese sandwich and never come back.

Alistair MacLeod (1936-2014), Canadian novelist

Of all the needs a book has, the chief need is that it be readable.

Anthony Trollope (1815-1882), prolific novelist, attended both Harrow and Winchester, fellow of New College, Oxford

REJECTIONS

When A Hundred Years of Solitude [Gabriel Garcia Márquez] came out, it got no good reviews at all. Roll on three or four years and it becomes an unquestioned classic!

Doris Lessing (1919-2013), novelist and poet.
Nobel Prize for Literature in 2007

The Beatles were rejected by Decca.

The board game Monopoly was originally written off by Parker Brothers.

The first performance of Mozart's 'Marriage of Figaro' was booed in Vienna.

When the Impressionists first showed their work they were laughed at.

André Gide, working for Éditions Gallimard, turned down Proust's 'Swann's Way'.

James Joyce's 'Ulysses' had to be privately printed in France. And 'The Dubliners' went unpublished for ten years.

When Ford launched their Nova family car in South America, they had forgotten that '*no va*' means '*no go*'. The car flopped.

Tolkien had Lord of the Rings rejected so many times that he paid for the publication of the first volume himself.

Robert Pirsig was turned down by 121 publishers (which led to an entry in *Guinness World Records* as the best selling book rejected by the most publishers) for *Zen and the Art of Motorcycle Maintenance: An Inquiry into Values* (to give the book its full title). It was finally published by William Morrow in 1974 and went on to sell five million copies.

The Museum of Failure is in Helsingborg, Sweden. It includes coffee-flavoured Coca-Cola and 'Hot Rod', an attempt by Harley-Davidson to distill the essence of its motorbikes into a perfume.

After reading the pilot script of Fawlty Towers written by John Cleese and his then wife Connie Booth, Ian Main, BBC Television's Comedy Script Editor wrote to the head of Comedy and Light Entertainment: 'I'm afraid I thought this as dire as its title. It's a kind of "Prince of Denmark' of the hotel world. A collection of clichés and stock characters which I can't see being anything but a disaster'

Taken from 'Letters of Note' compiled by Shaun Usher, 2013

Some books are to be tasted, others to be swallowed, and some few to be chewed and digested.

Francis Bacon (1561-1626), barrister, scientist, author and statesman

This is not a novel to be tossed aside lightly, it should be thrown with great force.

Dorothy Parker (1893-1927), American poet, wit and satirist

To do a piece [a review] well takes a long time, and time is not a thing that I am eager to fling idly through life's transom window.

Gore Vidal (1925-2012), American novelist, screenwriter and Senator

Duff to Diana, 20 March 1916
My Darling, my friend failed me at the last moment, telephoning from Tunbridge Wells about a missed train, so I dined, thank God, alone and was thus able to think about you with more concentration all the evening through.

There was nothing so remarkable about my dinner as to distract my thoughts from their absorbing subject. My soup, which was new to me, was made out of a sturgeon's fins but tasted like inferior turtle; a slice of salmon was followed by a Bordeaux pigeon whose slim, not to say emaciated, figure, was to me a subject both of envy and regret. Hardly had I decided to emulate by every possible means that swiftly swallowed bird, when a perfectly mature Gorgonzola made me forget my vows of perpetual attenuation, and encouraged me to drink two glasses of port in order that a bottle of claret, which had already insinuated itself into the sweet dim recesses of my body might not remain there without company.

Since then – for I keep nothing from you – I have drunk coffee and read Swift, who was a very witty, clever chap but not good natured and happy hearted like you and me. A book of prose underneath a roof, a nice cold partridge, a bottle of Perrier Jouet (1907) and you, sitting very close beside me and doing anything in the world except singing, and I should ask, very politely, to be excused going to Paradise for the present. How strange it is that one is balked of Paradise at every turn by things going not quite right. Here am I under a roof, surrounded by books of prose, with Perrier Jouet (1907) within reach, but alas, you are dining out and alas, alas it is the close season for partridges. Thank God at least that my father devoted a small portion of an uncertain income, derived from curing people of unmentionable complaints, to the high object of having me taught to write, for how otherwise, in the name of heaven, should I spend the miserable hours that I pass out of your company?

Duff.

Duff to Diana, 21 July 1918 (from the front line)
Darling – I should be justified in not writing today as I have so little time for sleep but I can't sleep happy until I have written. We arrived here [the front line] last midnight and I slept until nearly three. It is now ten a.m. Two bottles of port arrived for me this morning, which cheered us up enormously especially as we had already received two bottles last night – the first we have seen for weeks. Wine Red's eyes glistened and he said 'With four bottles of port in hand I regard the day as won'. He doesn't drink whiskey, poor lamb, and has been having toothache, which combined with our rather uneasy and very muddy position had begun to depress him. We take it in turns to walk round which takes some time to do. I did it early this morning – from five to eight. The morning began with clouds and a shower – the kind of morning Milton thinks of in Il Penseroso – and

then the sun came out fitfully but very prettily through the clouds, making strange yellow lights and the air smelt fresh and sweet, which it has not done lately. Also the larks sang as though they were mad with joy. I came back soon after eight and with great difficulty got one mug of water to shave and wash in, which means one less mug of water to drink till tomorrow night. And now I am having a glass of port and writing to you and waiting till 11 when I go on duty again. My feet are cold and wet and my legs are muddy but my hands are clean and my face is smooth, clean enough to touch your hands, smooth enough to kiss your face.

Duff.

*From 'A Durable Fire. The letters of **Duff Cooper**', 1984, edited by Artemis Cooper (daughter of JJ Norwich; married to Anthony Beevor; and half sister to Allegra Huston, mother of Angelica Huston)*

The light flowed out from the horns of the mountain, squeezed out laterally now, in a shaft of thin pencils, touching in the unsubstantial silhouettes of the fortresses and capes with a dream-like unreality. The terrace with its whitewashed walls was a glittering sun-trap, and here the old man brought me a single uncomfortable chair to sit on, above the hushing of the sea and the faint tingle of wind which snatched at the old Turkish pennant, holding and releasing it, blowing and lapsing. The long dusk began to settle with a shiver, and one of the silver peaks began to nibble the disc of travelling light – throwing a deep cool penumbra of shade into the valleys. Soon the light evening wind would be rushing across the Mesaoria to set the windmills turning in Nicosia; the homing yachts would flutter and tremble outside the Kyrenia bar; and Sabri on his little balcony at the police mess would glance at his watch and incline his cheek to take the breath as he sat contemplating the hard enamel of the water and the Turkish mountains huddled in shadow like a flock of sheep.

And the Abbey itself was there, fading in the last magnetic flush from the horizon, with its quiet groups of coffee-drinkers and card-players under the Tree of Idleness. At full moon we dined there, barefooted on the dark grass, to watch the lights winking away along the fretted coast and the great bronze coin shake itself free of the sunset-mist and climb with slow, perfectly punctuated steps into the nether heaven, bubbling into the great rose-window of the eastern wall like a visitant of the Gothic world. Here in the striped darkness, dotted with pools of luminous moonlight, we walked and talked, the smell of roses and wine and cigars mingling with the humbler scent of the limes, or the whiffs of bruised sage coming to us from the face of the mountain behind where Buffavento rose slowly to meet the moon, like a mailed fist. And somewhere upon the outer silence would come the haunting liquid music of a flute.

Lawrence Durrell (1912-1990), poet, dramatist, travel writer.
Married four times. From 'Bitter Lemons', 1971

Clouds drift, cherubim are on the wing, and swarms of putti, baptized in flight from the Greek Anthology, break loose over the tombs. They try on mitres and cardinals' hats and stumble under the weight of curtains and crosiers while stone Apostles and Doctors of the Church, who are really encyclopedists in fancy dress, gaze down indulgently. Female saints display the instruments of their martyrdom as light-heartedly as dice-boxes and fans. They are sovereign's favourites, landgravines dressed as naiads; and the androgynous saint-impersonating courtiers who ogle the ornate ceilings so meltingly from their plinths might all be acting in a charade. Sacred and profane change clothes and penitents turn into dominoes with the ambiguity of a masqued ball.

Concave and convex uncoil and pursue each other across the pilasters in ferny arabesques, liquid notions ripple, waterfalls running silver and blue drop to lintels and hang frozen there in curtains of artificial icicles. Ideas go feathering up in mock fountains and float away though the colonnades in processions of cumulus and cirrus. Light is distributed operatically and skies open in a new change of gravity that has lifted wingless saints and evangelists on journeys of aspiration towards three-dimensional sunbursts and left them levitated there, floating among cornices and spandrels and acanthus leaves and architectural ribands crinkled still with pleats from lying long folded in bandboxes.

Sir Patrick Leigh Fermor (1915-2011), travel writer, scholar and soldier.
From 'A Time of Gifts', 1977

Wandering in the back-lanes on the second day I was there, I went into a lively drinking-hall with the Magyar word vendeglö painted in large letters across the front pane and bumped into a trio of Hungarian farmers. Enmeshed in smoke and the fumes of plum-brandy with paprika-pods sizzling on the charcoal, they were hiccupping festive dactyls to each other and unsteadily clinking their tenth thimblefuls of palinka: vigorous, angular-faced, dark-clad and dark-glanced men with black moustaches tipped down at the corners of their mouths. Their white shirts were buttoned at the throat. They wore low-crowned black hats with narrow brims and high boots of shiny black leather with a Hessian notch at the knee. Hunnish whips were looped about their wrists. They might have just dismounted after sacking the palace of the Moravian kral.

My next call, only a few doors away, was a similar haunt of sawdust and spilt liquor and spit, but, this time, krma was daubed over the window. All was Slav within. The tow-haired Slovaks drinking there were dressed in conical fleece hats and patched sheepskin-jerkins with the matted wool turned inwards. They were shod in canoe-shaped cowhide moccasins. Their shanks, cross-gartered with uncured thongs, were bulbously swaddled in felt that would only be unwrapped in the spring. Swamp-and-conifer men they looked, with faces tundra-blank and eyes as blue and as vague as unmapped lakes which the plum-brandy was misting over.

Ibid

I hobbled round Linz by twilight. Pargeted façades rose up, painted chocolate, green, purple, cream and blue. They were adorned with medallions in high relief and the stone and plaster scroll-work gave them a feeling of motion and flow. Casemented half-hexagons jutted from the first storeys, and windowed three-quarter-cylinders blunted the corners, both of them soaring to the line of the eaves where they shelved into wasp-waists and re-expanded spherically to the same circumference, forming buoyant cupolas and globes; and domes and pinnacles and obelisks joined these decorative onions along the city's skyline. At ground-level, spiral commemorative columns rose twirling from the flagstones of the piazzas and hoisted radiating, monstrance-like, counter-Reformation bursts of gold spikes in mid-air. Except for the fierce keep on the rock, the entire town was built for pleasure and splendour. Beauty, space and amenity lay all about.

Ibid

In a soft, green valley where a stream ran through close-cropped, spongy pasture and the grass grew down below the stream's edge and merged there with the water-weeds; where a road ran between grass verges and tumbled walls, and the grass merged into moss which spread upwards and over the tumbled stones of the walls, outwards over the pocked metalling and deep ruts of the road; where the ruins of a police barracks, built to command the road through the valley, burnt in the troubles, had once been white, then black, and now were one green with the grass and the moss and the water-weed; where the smoke of burned turf drifted down from the cabin chimneys and joined the mist that rose from the damp, green earth; where the prints of ass and pig, goose and calf and horse mingled indifferently with those of barefoot children; where the soft, resentful voices rose and fell in the smoky cabins merging with the music of the stream and the treading and shifting and munching of the beasts at pasture; where mist and smoke never lifted and the sun never fell direct, and evening came slowly in infinite gradations of shadow; where the priest came seldom because of the rough road and the long climb home to the head of the valley, and no one except the priest ever came from one month's end to another, there stood an inn which was frequented in by-gone days by fishermen. Here in the summer nights when their sport was over they had sat long over their whisky and their pipes – professional gentlemen from Dublin and retired military men from England. No one fished the stream now and the few trout that remained were taken by ingenious and illicit means without respect for season or ownership. No one came to stay; sometimes a couple on a walking tour, once or twice a party of motorists, paused for supper, hesitated, discussed the matter and then regretfully pushed on to the next village. Here Ambrose came, perched on an outside-car, from the railway station over the hill six miles distant.

Evelyn Waugh (1903-1966), novelist, biographer, travel writer.
From 'Put Out More Flags', 1942

She was older, eighteen or nineteen, and had worn bright lipstick and sat down beside me in the warming house and slowly unlaced her leather boots and took them off and then her socks. My face turned red. In the Age of Imagination, before the Age of Full Disclosure, the removal of any article of clothing was inspirational. She was a cousin of the Ingqvists, up from Minneapolis for the Christmas break, and had a way about her that set her apart. Her hair, for example, was jet-black and cut short as a man's. She wore a short skirt and tights, but unlike other girls whose tights were lumpy from long johns, hers were tight. She leaned against me and said, 'Got a cigarette?' No girl asked me that before, because I didn't smoke, but for her sake, I said, 'Yeah', thinking I might have one – it certainly was worth a look, and who would say no at a time like that? – then said, 'Oh, I just remembered. I forgot mine at home'. She said, 'Oh well. I think I got two in my purse'. She offered one to me. I didn't smoke, but then I was young, I'd been held back, it was time to get started on these things, so I said, 'Thanks'. She gave me the book of matches. As I lit one and held it towards her mouth, she held my hand to steady it, and although I knew that you didn't make babies this way, two hands together holding a match, I thought it must be similar. We took deep drags and blew out big clouds of smoke, then she leaned back and inhaled again, and I leaned forward and put my head between my knees. Not sick exactly, I was simply appreciating it more than most people do. I was sixteen, I experienced everything deeply.

Garrison Keillor (b 1942), American storyteller, author and humorist.
From 'Lake Wobegone Days', 1985

He asked me the way to Bolsover street. I told him Bolsover street was in the middle of an intricate one-way system. It was a one-way system easy enough to get into. The only trouble was that, once in, you couldn't get out. I told him his best bet, if he really wanted to get to Bolsover street, was to take the first left, first right, second right, third on the left, keep his eye open for a hardware shop, go right round the square, keep to the inside lane, take the second Mews on the right and then stop. He will find himself facing a very tall office block, with a crescent courtyard. He can take advantage of this office block. He can go round the crescent, come out the other way, follow the arrows, go past two sets of traffic lights and take the next left indicated by the first green filter he comes across. He's got the Post Office Tower in his vision the whole time. All he's got to do is reverse into the underground park, change gear, go straight on, and he'll find himself in Bolsover street with no trouble at all.

Harold Pinter (b 1930). From 'No Man's Land', 1975

When I write a book I can devote as many hundreds or indeed thousands of words as I like to get into my readers' minds exactly how I want them to see my heroine. Should I be fool enough to write a play all I can write is 'Enter Millicent' and then I am in the hands of some damn tart who is sleeping with the manager.

Arnold Bennett (1867-1931), novelist and film screenwriter, on being asked why he had never written for the theatre

... writers have no game plan. 'You write what you enjoy.'

Sir Tom Stoppard (b 1937, Tomas Straussler), Czech born playwright and screenwriter.

Self-employed writers are paid 'per word, per piece or perhaps'.

Robert Benchley (1889-1945), American humourist and actor

One reason for writing, of course, is that no one's written what you want to read.

Philip Larkin (1922-1985), poet, novelist and librarian. Queen's Gold Medal for Poetry. Declined position of Poet Laureate.

... what I resent is that whenever you turn on the television you find people screaming at each other in their kitchens. People don't want to watch that. They want something different from their everyday lives. They want to see an attractive drawing room.

Dame Barbara Cartland (1901-2001), playwright, broadcaster and prolific author

Asking a working writer what he thinks about critics is like asking a lamp-post how it feels about dogs.

Christopher Hampton (b 1946), playwright and film director. Starred First in German and French at Oxford. (Sometimes attributed to John Osborne)

You can make a film about falling in love, you can make a film about falling out of love, but you can't make a film about being in love – too boring.

Sydney Pollack (1934-2008), American film director

A critic is a man who knows the way but can't drive a car.

Kenneth Tynan (1927-1980), controversial theatre critic and writer

Herbert Marshall was a British actor who made a name for himself in Hollywood during the 1930s despite losing a leg in World War I. He was between marriages when – or so the story has it – John Gielgud encountered him with the words: 'Ah, Herbert, I see you're foot-loose in Hollywood' .

Sir John Gielgud (1904-2000), actor and theatre director

When Gielgud told a theatrical company that all men must wear jock-straps under their leotards, a voice piped up: 'Please, Sir John, does that apply to those of us who only have small parts?'

Humphrey Bogart's all right until 11.30pm. After that, the trouble is, he thinks he's Humphrey Bogart.

Dave Chasen, Hollywood restaurateur

Oh well, you play Bach your way. I'll play him his.

Wanda Landowska (1879-1959), Polish harpsichordist, to fellow musician

It was three o'clock in the morning in New York. It was pouring with rain, and it came to me... 'And now the end is near and so I face the final curtain' ... And I said wow that's it, that's for Sinatra... and then I cried.

Paul Anka (b 1941), Canadian singer and songwriter, on completing the lyrics of 'My Way'

ROYAL CONCERT, ALBERT HALL

Your Majesty

Master Kenyon, overwhelmed by his inadequacy and by the feebleness of his mild expressions to convey the effect of Wednesday evening's concert, has laid down his pen so that I, after the passage of ten score years since I recorded the first Commemoration of the incomparable Handel, might take it up once again.

I have heard tell, by those whose report I fear is less than trustworthy, that there are those who disdain in Your age to hear this pleasing, grand and sublime music with many choirs of voices and assemblies of instruments, shunning the thunder of the drums, the tread of the double basses, and the noise of the grand organ. Yet it may safely be pronounced that, from the progress which practical Music has made in this country since Handel's time, his work was never so well performed under his own direction as it was on Wednesday evening under the distinguished Sir David Willcocks and Mr Meredith Davies.

How aptly he wrote who asked a century ago: 'Who ever heard of a choir too large for Handel? Not though nations should be formed into choirs and the genius of thunder were to swell the harmony till it shook the very spheres, would the true votary of Handel cry "Hold, enough!"'. The aggregate of voices and instruments had here its full effect, and near a thousand musicians in the immortal choruses of 'Israel in Egypt' and 'The Messiah' made it difficult to determine which was the best, or had the grandest effect, from the very uncommon force and accuracy with which they were now performed.

And yet more notable than the glorious numbers of the performers was their extreme youth, for as I was informed they are but fledgling members of the newly formed colleges of music under your protection. How near, or how distant, the time may be, when the art of combining sounds shall be brought to its highest perfection by the natives of Great Britain, this is not the place to enquire; but progress has been sure.

He must have been not only a fastidious, but a very ignorant and insensible hearer who did not receive new and exquisite pleasure from the execution of Ariodante's sublime aria 'Dopo notte' by Dame Janet Baker, and from the sober beauty of Miss Lott and Mr Roberts, though I believe I might prefer the noted talents of Mr Nicolai Gedda to be heard in our Italian opera houses.

I am, with the most profound Humility, Your Majesty's most dutiful and devoted Subject and Servant,

*After **Dr Charles Burney** (1726-1814), musicologist and composer.*

The Times, 23 November 1984

I'm using tons of steel to make things look lighter.

Richard Serra (b 1938), American-Spanish sculptor working with monumental steel structures

... as when heaved anew,
Old ocean rolls a lengthened wave to shore
Down whose green back the short lived foam, all hoar,
Bursts gradual, with a wayward indolence.

John Keats (1795-1821), Romantic poet, trained as a doctor

The ocean is becoming rough; the waves come in slowly, tugging strength from far back. The moment before they somersault, the moment when they arch their backs so beautifully, showing green and white veins amid the black, that moment is intolerable. They finally crack, dashing directly upon the sand, actually driving, full force downward against the sand, bouncing upward and forward, and at last petering out into a small stream which races up the beach and is then recalled.

Delmore Schwartz (1913-1966), Romanian-American poet and writer. From the short story 'In Dreams Begin Responsibilities'

Soon she struggled to a certain hill-top, and saw far before her the silent inflooding of the day. Out of the east it welled and whitened; the darkness trembled into light; and the stars were extinguished like the street lights of a human city. The whiteness brightened into silver, the silver warmed into gold, the gold kindled into pure and living fire; and the face of the east was burned with elemental scarlet. The day drew its first long breath, steady and chill; and for leagues around the woods sighed and shivered.

RL Stevenson (1850-1894), novelist, poet and travel writer. From 'Prince Otto', 1885

Riders are tiny against cliffs. A figure, anonymous in the blurring light, waves from the immense shoulder of a rock... a streaked indifferent red sky leans over a plain where suddenly, far off, birds fly up and dust swirls.

Dilys Powell (1901-1995), film critic and journalist. Starred First in modern languages at Oxford. From her review, in 1956, of the John Ford film 'The Searchers', starring John Wayne

I know a garden where roses and lilies bloom
The choking weeds a challenge to remove.
Where joy and grief walk hand in hand;
And love is there.

I know a manor where the rooms are filled with beauty
And dust and time stand still in harmony;
And commoners may sit with kings;
And love is there.

I know a meadow where the skylark sings
In golden morning light and evening glow;
And paradise is all around to see;
And love is there.

I know a garden where fond memory
Holds the door for ever open, and peace
On fluttering wings brings calm to all who enter;
And love is there.

Written by friend of Bea Wilsey about Maufant Manor, our Jersey home from 1980 to 1989

Having agreed to see a production of one of his plays at Bury St Edmonds, Noel Coward was invited to attend a service commemorating the saint who gave his name to the town. He declined thus: 'I came to Bury St Edmonds, not to praise him.'

John Betjeman was in the audience at a lecture given by Lord David Cecil on the pleasures of reading. After the lecture, Cecil expressed his surprise to Betjeman at seeing him there. Betjeman replied that he had been misled. He had expected the lecture to be about the pleasures of Reading.

John Betjeman (born Betjemann) (1906-1984) poet, writer and broadcaster. Founded the Victorian Society. Poet Laureate 1972

'The setting was familiar. The lights were low, the spotlight was pink, the air was reeking, the dawn was in the East, and Miss Traubel was dew-pearled. She hated, as the song prescribes, to see the evening sun go down. But it was the petulance of a hostess who commands flocks of servants but cannot control a short circuit in the chandelier.

Miss Traubel sang on pitch. She swayed like a riven oak over her failure to compete with 'powder and store-bought hair' – a likely story. She rocked her alabaster shoulders in a two-four rhythm to assert her oneness with the common people.

… once a prima donna has experienced the guilty thrill of singing 'She done tole me don't wear no black', illiteracy must take on in her off-hours the powerful appeal that buttermilk has for a professional champagne taster.

Miss Traubel is now an addict of that good old 'sweet and low down', and her indignation at Mr Bing* knows no bounds. She has published, without Mr Bing's permission, an exchange of letters with him. They may never be embalmed with quite the reverence of the Shaw–Terry correspondence but they provide equally instructive lessons in the first principles of art and life.

Mr Bing referred to her Chicago appearance and reasoned rather uneasily that 'I could so well understand that these two activities [opera and jazz] do not really seem to mix very well'. In fairness to Miss Traubel it should be said that she never suggested sneaking 'Ain't Misbehavin'' into Tristan. 'Perhaps,' reflected Mr Bing, who has a pretty talent for intimidation, 'you would prefer to give the Metropolitan a miss for a year or so until you may possibly feel that you want again to change back to the more serious aspects of your art.

Miss Traubel was too mad to bother returning these subjunctives and conditionals. 'Artistic dignity is not a matter of where one sings,' she laid

---

Rudolf Bing, Chief General Manager, New York Metropolitan Opera

down. 'The artist of integrity who refuses to compromise her standards is able to imbue whatever places she appears in with dignity.'

Alistair Cooke (1908-2004), broadcaster of 'Letter from America' for 58 years, from 'America Observed', 1988

He was a tall young man and he would bend his right knee laterally, his right foot resting upon an inward-pointing toe. He had retreating shoulders, a retreating forehead, a retreating waist. The face itself was a curved face, a boneless face, a rather pink face, fleshy about the chin. His eyelashes were fair and fluttering; his lips were full. When he giggled, which he did with nervous frequency, his underlip would come to rest below his upper teeth. He held his cigarette between the index and the middle fingers, keeping them outstretched together with the gesture of a male impersonator puffing at a cigar. His hands, rather damp on their inner side, gave the impression on their outer side of being double-jointed. He dressed simply, wearing an opal pin, and a velours hat tilted angularly. He had a peculiar way of speaking: his sentences came in little splashing pounces; and then from time to time he would hang on to a word as if to steady himself: he would say 'Simplytooshattering for words,' the phrase being a slither with a wild clutch at the banister of 'for'. He was very shy.

Sir Harold Nicholson (1886-1968), on Lambert Orme, from 'Some People'. The book characterised real people and Orme is known to be Ronald Firbank (1886-1926), a novelist and university contemporary

Humphrey Littleton on Lionel Blair's mood swings on his return to pantomime for Snow White: 'One moment he's feeling Happy and the next he has come all over Grumpy'.

Humphrey 'Humph' Littleton (1921-2008), Old Etonian jazz trumpeter, broadcaster and cartoonist. I'm Sorry I Haven't a Clue, July 2007. Lionel Blair, born Henry Lionel Ogus, (b 1931), actor, choreographer and tap dancer. Degree in Ethnography.

'We keep Nigel's book in the downstairs loo.'

'Do you really? There can't be many pages left.'

Anon

We all have a dark feeling of resistance towards people we have never met, and a profound and manly dislike of the authors we have never read.

GK Chesterton (1874-1936), theologian, poet, dramatist and art critic

Then, silence. Some fancied they heard in the air
A weary and wandering sigh
That sounded like '–jum!' but the others declare
It was only a breeze that went by.

*Lewis Carroll, born Charles Lutwidge Dodgson (1832-1898),
writer, mathematician, Anglican deacon and photographer.
From 'The Hunting of the Snark', 1876*

*Baroness James of Holland, better known as **PD James** (1920-2014), and the author of many crime novels died in 2014. On Desert Island Discs, one of her stories concerned a book signing in Sydney. 'To Emma Chizzit', she wrote with a smile – only for it to dawn on her that the customer had been enquiring about the price.*

When the first toast was called, he rose and in the name of the whole company addressed me for a full quarter of an hour with a warmth of feeling, a wealth of ideas and a turn of phrase which many orators would envy. I was deeply touched. Unhappily, if he spoke well, he drank likewise.

That fatal cup set such tides of champagne flowing that all Liszt's eloquence was shipwrecked in it. Belloni and I were still reasoning with him in the street at two in the morning, and urging on him the advisability of waiting until daylight before engaging in single combat with pistols at two yards' range with a Bohemian who had drunk even better than he.

Hector Berlioz (1803-1869), recalling an after dinner speech by Liszt

They decided to bury him in our churchyard at Greymede under the beeches; the widow would have it so, and nothing might be denied her in her state.

It was magnificent morning in early spring when I watched among the trees to see the procession come down the hillside. The upper air was woven with the music of the larks, and my whole world thrilled with the conception of summer. The young pale windflowers had arisen by the wood-gale, and under the hazels, when perchance the hot sun pushed his way, new little suns dawned, and blazed with real light. There was a certain thrill and quickening everywhere, as a woman must feel when she has conceived. A sallow tree in a favoured spot looked like a pale gold cloud of summer dawn; nearer it had poised a golden, fairy busby on every twig, and was voiced with a hum of bees, like any sacred golden bush, uttering its gladness in the thrilling murmur of bees, and in warm scent. Birds called and flashed on every hand; they made off exultant with streaming strands of grass, or wisps of fleece, plunging into the dark spaces of the wood, and out again into the blue.

DH Lawrence (1885-1930), novelist, poet and playwright.
From 'The White Peacock', 1911

The Bloomsbury Set attracted a number of middle class literati and artists in the first decade of the 20th century who believed in the importance of art. With their modern attitudes towards feminism, pacifism and sexuality they became an influential group. Amongst them were Vanessa Bell, Duncan Grant, Clive Bell, Virginia Woolf, EM Forster, Roger Fry, John Maynard Keynes and Lytton Strachey. Dorothy Parker summed them up: 'They lived in squares, painted in circles, loved in triangles.'

I have lost the attributions of the following imaginative descriptions:

The waiter had an apron soft with old dirt, strands of hair were arranged across his scalp like oily ribbons and his fingers were like toes.

Something was coming, like a train made of wind.

As the first grey light of morning leaked into the arid Sinai desert, it spread a shimmer of divine glory...

The wild night whispers your name.

He flung himself into the chair which groaned in dismay.

She would have suited the role of Brittania or Columbia in a patriotic display. She was massive, cumbersome and statuesque and towered above her husband like a skyscraper above a shack, but when he talked, and he did so with vivacity and wit, her heavy features relaxed into a fond smile.

Her mouth was as shiny as jam.

I do not know how to write poetically, I am no poet. I do not know how to distribute my phrases so that they cast shadows and light, I am no painter. Nor do I know how to express my feelings, my thoughts with gestures and mime, I am no dancer. But I can do all this with notes, because I am a musician.

Wolfgang Amadeus Mozart (1756-1791)

He snatched the lightning from the skies and the sceptre from the tyrants.

Anne-Robert-Jacques Turgot, Baron Laune (1727-1781),
following the death of Benjamin Franklin (1706-1790)

Literature used to be about having sex and not much about children. Life is the other way round.

David Lodge (b 1935), author, literary critic and playwright

A Grandmother is a lady who has no children of her own, so she likes other people's children. Grandmothers don't have anything to do but be there. They are old so they shouldn't play or run. They should never say 'Hurry up'. Usually they are fat but not too fat to tie children's shoes. They wear

glasses and funny underwear and they can take their teeth and gums out. They don't have to be smart, only answer questions like why dogs hate cats and why God isn't married. They don't talk baby-talk like visitors do. When they read to us they don't skip bits or mind if it is the same story over again. Everyone should have one, especially if you don't have television, because grandmothers are the only grown-ups who have time.

A six year old

A TALE OF TWO CITIES

by Charles Dickens

Doctor released,
Marquis deceased,
Darnay acquitted,
Monarchy submitted,
Marriage announced,
Darnay denounced,
Places are switched,
Blades are twitched,
Seamstress cries,
Carton dies.

Liz Coppla

---

20 Cavendish Square, 4 August 1905
I have never been here in August before, and I don't suppose you have either: you can't conceive the dreary, drooping, deflowered, depopulated morning-after-the-ball appearance which it presents – the sickening miasma of stale smoke, dead violets, dusty rooms, melting butter, tinned food, drunken servants, sleepy cabmen and exhausted members of the White Hungarian Band – everywhere the ashes and odours of yesterday's debauch.

To Mrs Homer, 10 October 1905
I shoot by myself on the tops of the hills and read Ovid in front of the fire – very agreeable after the congestion of fools that we have had here for the last 10 days. All the best bedrooms have been filled with the valets of the greatest bores in Britain, and the only big bath always occupied by the chauffeur of my father's wine merchant – just because he plays bridge and voted against the government on the Irish Supply – the merchant I mean, the chauffeur didn't even do that, and he drives damnably.

To Katherine Asquith, 23 July 1910
Couldn't we, by the way, have called the baby Yelling? It struck me as rather a good name when I read it in yesterday's Times – it appears that Detmar Blow, the architect, is the third son of the late Yelling Blow. (One might even be called Howling Gale.) Could you enquire whether it is a girl's name or only a boy's? And do you think that Mary Yelling Asquith or Yelling Mary Asquith sounds better?

Raymond Asquith (1878-1916), barrister, to Katherine Homer (his future wife). From 'Letters of Raymond Asquith' by John Jolliffe, 1987

Conchita Marin was a careless, spirited and heavy-breasted woman with two sons and no husband. Her lovers had fish-scales on their jerseys and came in fresh from the sea. The morning I called on her, she had on a pink jumper, jingly earings and an uncommon amount of green eye-paint. A few plastic curlers were trying to establish order in her tangle of black hair.

Bruce Chatwin (1940-1967), novelist, journalist, travel writer and art advisor. From 'In Patagonia', 1977

She was waiting for me, a white face behind a dusty window. She smiled, her painted mouth unfurling as a red flag caught in a sudden breeze. Her hair was dyed dark-auburn. Her legs were a mesopotamia of varicose veins. She still had the tatters of an extraordinary beauty.

At some negative turning point she had married a moon-faced Swede.

They joined two failures in one and drifted towards the end of the world. Caught by chance in this eddy, they built the perfect cottage of his native Malmö, with its intelligent windows and vertical battens painted red with iron-oxide.

Ibid

Books are the liberated spirits of men and should be bestowed in a heaven of light and grace, harmonious colour and sumptuous comfort.

Mark Twain (1935-1910). First lines of his speech on the inaurguration of the Millicent Library, Fairhaven, Massachusetts (1893)

Said Hamlet to Ophelia,
'I'll do a sketch of thee,
What kind of pencil shall I use,
2B or not 2B?'

Terence 'Spike' (after Spike Jones) Milligan (1918-2002), comedian, writer and actor. Son of Captain Alphonso Milligan. Educated at St Paul's, Rangoon

If it sounds like writing, I will rewrite it.

Elmore Leonard Jr (1925-2013), American novelist and screenwriter. One of his Rules of Writing. Known as The Dickens of Detroit

I have been told that Wagner's music is better than it sounds.
Edgar Wilson Nye (1850-1896). American journalist

I'm a marvellous housekeeper. Every time I leave a man, I keep his house.

When asked how many husbands she had had, she replied "Other than my own?"

Zsa Zsa Gabor (born Sari Gabor)(1917-2016) Hungarian/American actress, socialite and serial wife (nine husbands)

It's like holding a candle. Beautiful, exciting but you are never sure when it will go out.

Conrad Hilton (1887-1979) American hotelier (188 hotels in 38 countries). On being married to Zsa Zsa Gabor (the second of nine husbands)

In 1955, the violinist George Enesco was persuaded to take part in a concert, in which he accompanied on the piano a young man whom he had been teaching the violin (a reluctant teaching assignment brought about by a favour owed to the young man's father). At the concert, Enesco's friend, the pianist Alfred Cortot, volunteered to turn the music pages.

Next day, the music critic of Le Figaro wrote: "There was a strange concert at the Salle Gareau last night. The man whom we adore when he plays the violin, played the piano; another whom we adore when he plays the piano, turned the pages and a man who should have been turning the pages, played the violin.

George Enesco (1881-1955) Romanian composer, violinist, pianist, conducter and teacher. Vienna Conservatoire aged 7. Married Princess Cantacuzino

Alfred Cortot (1877-1962) Swiss-French pianist and conducter. Recorded more Chopin than any other pianist

CONSTRUCTION INSTRUCTION

As the architect detailed it

As the structural engineer designed it

As the surveyor priced for it

As the project co-ordinator visualised it

As the contractor built it

What the client wanted

A doctor can bury his mistakes but an architect can only advise his client to plant climbing vines.

Frank Lloyd Wright (1897-1959), American architect, writer and interior designer. Founder of the Prairie Style of Usonian architecture

My only job is to stay well so that I can show up and be charming.

Kirk Douglas (b 1916), born Issur Danielovitch to illiterate Russian peasants. Professional wrestler, US navy, film actor (90 films). On his 100th birthday

Green with lust and sick with shyness,
Let me lick your lacquered toes.
Gosh, oh gosh, your Royal highness,
Put your finger up my nose,
Pin my teeth upon your dress,
Plant my head with watercress.
Only you can make me happy.
Tuck me tight beneath your arm.
Wrap me in a woollen nappy;
Let me wet it till it's warm.
In a plush and plated pram
Wheel me round St James's, Ma'am.
Let your sleek and soft galoshes
Slide and slither on my skin.
Swaddle me in mackintoshes
Till I lose my sense of sin.
Lightly plant your plimsolled heel
Where my privy parts congeal.

Satire by Sir Maurice Bowra (1898-1971), (classical scholar, literary critic, academic and wit. Double first at Oxford) on his friend Sir John Betjeman (1906-1984) (poet, writer and broadcaster. Founder of Victorian Society, Poet Laureate. Failed even a Third at Oxford. Bisexual) who was choked with emotion on being presented with the Duff Cooper Prize by Princess Margaret.

I imagine Paradise will be a kind of library.

Jorge Louis Borges (1899-1986) Argentinian writer, poet and philosopher.
Blind by aged 55. Trilingual Spanish, English, German

Over the door of the Library of Thebes is the inscription:

MEDICINE FOR THE SOUL

Quoted by **Diodorus Siculus.** *Greek historian, born in Sicily*

How still and peaceful is a library. It seems quiet as a grave, tranquil as heaven, a cool collection of the thoughts of men of all times. Yet, open the pages and you will find dissention and disputes, alive with abuse and detraction; a huge, many-volumed satire upon man, written by himself. What a broad thing is a library, all shapes of opinion reflected on its catholioc bosom, as sunbeams and shadows upon the ample mirror of a lake.

George Gilfillan (1813-1878) Scottish author and poet

Libraries are the wardrobes of literature

George Dryer

To me, poor man, my library
Was dukedom large enough.

Shakespeare. The Tempest

The historian will tell you what happened. The novelist will tell you what it felt like.

EL Doctorow (1931-2015) American novelist

A painter has so much more talent when he is dead.

*Samuel Langhorne Clemens, known as **Mark Twain** (1835-1910)*
American writer, humorist and publisher

Two things in that play need to be cut. The second act and that child's throat.

Noel Coward *(1899-1973) Playwright, actor, entertainer.*
Attributed to watching 14 year old Bonnie Langford.

5 | Poetry and Lyrics

Cleere had the day bin from the dawne,
All chequerd was the Skye,
Thin clouds like Scarfs of Cobweb Lawne
Valyd Heaven's most glorious eye.
The Winde had no more strength than this,
That leasurely it blew,
To make one leafe the next to kisse,
That closely by it grew.

Michael Drayton (1563-1631), Elizabethan poet.
From 'The Sixt Nimphall', 1630

Till now the doubtful dusk reveal'd
The knolls once more where, couch'd at ease,
The white kine glimmer'd, and the trees
Laid their dark arms about the field:

And suck'd from out the distant gloom
A breeze began to tremble o'er
The large leaves of the sycamore,
And fluctuate all the still perfume,

And gathering freshlier overhead,
Rock'd the full-foliaged elms, and swung
The heavy-folded rose, and flung
The lilies to and fro, and said

'The dawn, the dawn,' and died away;
And East and West, without a breath,
Mixt their dim lights, like life and death,
To broaden into boundless day.

Lord Alfred Tennyson (1809-1892). From 'In Memoriam', 1850

But when the fields are still,
And the tired men and dogs all gone to rest,
And only the white sheep are sometimes seen
Cross and recross the strips of moon-blanch'd green;
Come, shepherd, and again renew the quest.

Matthew Arnold (1822-1888), poet, one-time schools inspector.
From 'The Scholar Gypsy', 1853

JR'S 40TH BIRTHDAY PARTY, 2 JANUARY 1981

He began his career as a soldier
He followed it up as a guide,
Then showing a taste for fair women
He took Miss McKay as his bride.

They trotted in harness to Chelsea,
They tethered in Paultons Street,
Fenella and Candida joined them
And they drove on to rustic retreat.

So what then became of our Jamie?
Whose history we have just spun;
Steel yourselves for news of the present,
Now that good years have begun!

He talks like William of Wykeham;
And he cooks like Escoffier.
He looks like a matinée idol,
(Or that's what the sycophants say).
He lives in a Georgian hovel, –
Adjoining allotment as well,
Where there's tennis and croquet and swimming.
How can he endure such pure hell?

By giving with generous abandon
To all of his friends and his blades
The treasure of some of his talents
He's sure to survive more decades.

Chris Lumb (b 1943), *linguist, lyricist, musician, and*
Godfrey Carey (b 1942), *Queen's Counsel*

My generous parents-in-law gave me a case of Glenmorangie whisky each Christmas.

Glenmorangie, Glenmorangie;
That potpourri of fragrancy,
A whisky at its apogee,
The alchemy of poetry.
The therapy of lethargy.

Glenmorangie, Glenmorangie;
Facsimile of bonhomie,
'Le dernier cri' of duty free,
A symphony of harmony.
Epiphany most 'sans souci'.

Glenmorangie, Glenmorangie;
While liquid honey you may be,
Frequency will 'perdre des esprits'.
Too many tipples topples me
I will be 'allé au tapis'.

The moral is quite plain to see:
While eulogy is up to three
Elegy is more than six.

JRC, Val d'Isère, April 1986. (Perhaps influenced
by the French spoken all around!)

A SETTLER'S POEM

It rained and rained and rained.
The average fall was well maintained
And when the tracks were simple bogs,
It started raining cats and dogs.
After a drought of half an hour
We had a most refreshing shower
And then, most dampening yet of all,
A drenching rain began to fall.
Next day but one was fairly dry
Save for one deluge from the sky
Which wetted the party to the skin;
And then at last the rain set in.

Glenorchy Museum, South Island, New Zealand

THAT'S AMORE

When the moon hits your eye
Like a big pizza pie
That's amore.

When an eel bites your hand
And that's not what you planned
That's a moray.

When our habits are strange
And our customs deranged
That's our mores.

When your horse munches straw
And the bales total four
That's some more hay.

When a Japanese knight
Waves his sword in a fight
That's Samurai.

When Othello's poor wife
She gets strangled in strife
That's a Moor, eh?

When your sheep go to graze
In a damp marshy place,
That's a moor, eh?

When you ace your last test
Like you did all the rest
That's some more As!

When on Mount Cook you see
A tall aborigine,
That's a Maori.

When you've had quite enough
Of this dumb rhyming stuff
That's no more! Eh?

Jack Brooks (1912-1971), (also 'Wagon Train', 'Ole Buttermilk Sky') and Harry Warren (1893-1981), American composer, lyricist, and triple Oscar winner. Wrote over 800 songs and the musical '42nd Street'

Miss Twy was soaping her breasts in the bath
When behind her she heard a sinister laugh.
Turning around she then discovered
A naughty man in the bathroom cupboard.

First published poem (while still at Wellington College) of Louis MacNiece (1907-1963), Irish poet and playwright

Mark my words, when a society has to resort to the lavatory
for its humour, the writing is on the wall.

Alan Bennett (b 1934), playwright, screen writer, actor, author, Russian speaker, First Class history degree from Oxford. Original member of Beyond the Fringe

THE VIOLIN

A sycamore tree cannot mimic the lark.
A sycamore tree's unaccompanied bark
Is silent until the tree's finally felled.
Seasoned and shaped and then lovingly held
Beneath a Korean or Hungarian chin.
A sycamore's what makes a great violin.

A sheep cannot sing. The song of a sheep
Would shatter a goblet, or rouse you from sleep –
But the guts of a sheep when a sheep's passed away
Can be twisted and tightened and tuned to an A.
So what started off filling up a sheep's middle
Ends up as strings on the sycamore fiddle.

Now a horse cannot sing you a musical scale
But if you sneak up and you shorten his tail
The hairs, when attached to a suitable rod,
Can play the sheep's guts like the song of a God.
The rest of the horse, if it's under the weather,
Is boiled up to glue the whole violin together.

So if you should pass by a meadow or lea
Where a sheep grazes next to a sycamore tree
And yonder a horse canters tail in the air,
You will know the true meaning beneath what lies there.
You can say to the kids with a wave of your arm,
'What you see over there is a violin farm'.

Sir Richard Stilgoe (b 1943), song writer, lyricist
('Phantom of the Opera', 'Starlight Express') and musician.
Member of Cambridge University Footlights

THE THREE-LEGGED PIG

As I set out for a walk one day
I saw a pig in a sty.
I looked in as the pig lay there
And I swear that it's no lie,
The pig had only three legs
And where the fourth should be
Was a hand-carved peg leg made from brass
And tipped with ivory.

Well, the farmer he came passing by
And I said 'Farmer tell to me,
How come that pig instead of four legs
Has now got only three'.
He scratched his head with a pitchfork
And sat down on a log,
Saying 'Son, I've got to tell you
That's no ordinary hog!'

Two years last Spring, the old school bus
On the hill it lost its brakes
Chock full of kids, shot down the hill
And then went into the lake.
The kids were crying; thought they were dying
But the pig into the lake it dived
Pulled every kid out and with its snout
Gave them the kiss of life.

Last Summertime, my grandchild,
(A child just one year old)
Was playing by the railway and wandered on the line.
The express came by, I thought he'd die,
All we could do was pray.
But while we were crying, the pig went flying
And dragged the child away.

'Old farmer', I said, 'I've got to thank you
For the story of the wonderful pig.
Wherever I go, I'll let folks know
Of the wonderful things he did.
But that still doesn't explain the peg leg'.
The farmer said 'You dunce, –
After all that pig had done,
We couldn't eat him all at once!'.

Quoted by **Mike Harding** *'The Rochdale Cowboy' (b 1944),*
singer, songwriter, comedian and instrumentalist.
On 'Start the Week', Radio 4, November 1984.

CLERIHEWS

The art of Biography
Is different from Geography.
Geography is about maps,
Biography is about chaps.

Sir Humphry Davy
Abominated gravy.
He lived in the odium
Of having discovered sodium.

Sir Christopher Wren
Said, 'I am going to dine with some men.
If anybody calls,
Say I am designing St Paul's'.

E Clerihew Bentley *(1875-1956). Clerihew was his mother's maiden*
name. Educated at St Paul's. President of Oxford Union. Called to
the Bar 1901. Daily Telegraph leader writer for 22 years

William Blake
Found Newton hard to take,
And was not enormously taken
With Francis Bacon.

WH Auden (1907-1973), Anglo-American poet

Cecil B de Mille
Rather against his will,
Was persuaded to leave Moses
Out of The Wars of the Roses.

Nicolas Bentley (son of ECB) (1907-1978), illustrator

Miss Mae West
Is one of the best;
I would rather not
Say the best what.

EW Fordham (d 1956), barrister

In Australia,
Inter alia,
Mediocrities
Think they're Socrates.

Sheridan Morley (1941-2007), biographer, critic and broadcaster

Henry James
(Whatever his claims)
Is not always deuced
Lucid.

Clifton Fadiman (1904-1999), American broadcaster and author

WOAD OF HARLECH

Romans came across the Channel
All wrapped up in tin and flannel.
Half a pint of woad per man'll
Clothe you more than these.

Saxon hordes when bent on slaughter
Wore pyjamas which were water-
Tight, but every soldier caught a
Batch of lice or fleas.

Tramp up Snowdon with your woad on
Never mind if you get snowed on
Never need a button sewed on.
We are men of woad!

What's the use of wearing braces,
Vests and pants and boots with laces,
Spats and hats you buy in places
Like Forsyth's or Maude's.

What's the use of shirts of cotton,
Studs that always get forgotten.
Such affairs are simply rotten.
Better far with woad!

Woad's the stuff to show, men!
Woad to scare your foemen!
Boil it to a brilliant blue
And rub it on your back and your abdomen.

Ancient Britons never hit on
Anything as good as woad to fit on
Knees or neck or where you sit on;
Tailors, you be blowed.

William Hope-Jones, Eton housemaster.
Quoted from memory by Sinclair Dunnett, Scottish wildlife guide,
as we sailed down the River Niger in Mali, November 2002.

HIGH FLIGHT

Oh! I have slipped the surly bonds of earth
And danced the skies on laughter-silvered wings;
Sunward I've climbed, and joined the tumbling mirth
Of sun-split clouds – and done a hundred things
You have not dreamed of – wheeled and soared and swung
High in the sunlit silence. Hov'ring there
I've chased the shouting wind along, and flung
My eager craft through footless halls of air.
Up, up the long delirious, burning blue,
I've topped the windswept heights with easy grace
Where never lark, or even eagle flew –
And, while with silent lifting mind I've trod
The high untrespassed sanctity of space,
Put out my hand and touched the face of God.

*Pilot Officer **Gillespie Magee** (1922-1941), Anglo-American aviator*
and poet. Educated at Rugby and served in Canadian Air Force

If thou art tired and sore behet
With troubles that thou would'st forget
Take to the trees and hills.
No tears can dim the sweet happiness
That nature wears.

*   **Henry Longfellow** *(1807-1882), American poet.*
First to translate Dante's 'The Divine Comedy'

The mountain sheep are sweeter
But the valley sheep are fatter
We therefore deemed it meeter
To carry off the latter.

Thomas Love Peacock *(1785-1866), Novelist and poet.*
Director of East India Company

I was so much older then
I'm younger than that now.

*Bob Dylan (born Robert Zimmerman) (b 1941),
American singer-songwriter. From 'My Back Pages', 1967*

The bells they sound on Bredon,
And still the steeples hum.
'Come all to church, good people,' –
Oh, noisy bells, be dumb;
I hear you, I will come.

*AE Housman (1859-1936), poet and classical scholar.
Last verse of 'Bredon Hill'*

To see a World in a grain of sand,
And a heaven in a wild flower,
Hold Infinity in the palm of your hand,
And Eternity in an hour.

William Blake (1757-1827), painter, poet and printmaker

There's a breathless hush in the Close to-night –
Ten to make and the match to win –
A bumping pitch and a binding light,
An hour to play and the last man in.
And it's not for the sake of a ribboned coat,
Or the selfish hope of a season's fame,
But his Captain's hand on his shoulder smote –
'Play up! Play up! And play the game!'

The sand of the desert is sodden red, –
Red with the wreck of a square that broke; –
The Gatling's jammed and the Colonel dead,
And the river of death has brimmed his banks
And England's far and Honour a name,

But the voice of a schoolboy rallies the ranks:
"Play up! Play up! And play the game!"

Henry Newbolt (1862-1938), poet, novelist, historian. From 'Vitai Lampada' (The Torch of Life). The engagement described in verse two is of the Battle of Abu Klea in the Sudan in January 1885. It was an unsuccessful attempt to rescue General Gordon. The colonel is Frederick Burnaby, a swashbuckling army officer and linguist

WILTSHIRE v THE REST

Poor weary Londoner, come to the fresh green countryside,
To the hush of the grass growing under the deck chair,
To the peace of the shadowing branches and the rest of roses.
Come, come away from that thundering city of lights,
And lie in the silent sun, in the calm of a long week-end.
All is quiet here: on Saturday there are only four to lunch,
And five to tea, and six to drinks, and seven to dinner,
And eight coming in afterwards to play Canasta till dawn.
On Sunday there are only nine people dropping in after church,
And ten of us going to look at a wonderful garden
Which is only eleven miles away, in the afternoon.
There may be twelve coming in for supper, but you can leave early
And catch the midnight train which gets in at two,
So do come and relax, you poor tired thing with your pale face,
Come to our peaceful, restful, hushful, quiet countryside.

Virginia Graham. On the bedroom wall of a B&B in Great Bedwyn, Wiltshire

It matters not how strait the gate,
How charged the punishments the scroll,
I am the master of my fate:
I am the captain of my soul.

William Ernest Henley (1849-1903), editor and poet. Left leg amputated as a result of tuberculosis and three years in hospital; then a model for Stevenson's Long John Silver. From 'Invictus', 1888

*The obscure, absurd and delightful humorous poems of **Patrick Barrington**, 11th Viscount Barrington of Ardglass (1908-1990) have always amused me. This Irish peer seems to have done little else than dream up the fantastical and improbable. Here are two:*

THE DIPLOMATIC PLATYPUS

I had a duck-billed platypus when I was up at Trinity,
With whom I soon discovered a remarkable affinity.
He used to live in lodgings with myself and Arthur Purvis,
And we all went up together for the Diplomatic Service.
Our summary rejection, though we took it with urbanity
Was naturally wounding in some measure to our vanity;
The bitterness of failure was considerably mollified,
However, by the ease with which our platypus had qualified.
The wisdom of the choice, it soon appeared, was undeniable;
There never was a diplomat more thoroughly reliable.
He never made rash statements his enemies might hold him to,
He never stated anything, for no one ever told him to,
And soon he was appointed, so correct was his behaviour,
Our Minister (without Portfolio) to Trans-Moravia.
My friend was loved and honoured from the Andes to Estonia,
He soon achieved a pact between Peru and Patagonia,
He never vexed the Russians nor offended the Rumanians,
He pacified the Letts and yet appeased the Lithuanians.
When on the Anniversary of Greek Emancipation,
Alas! He laid an egg in the Bulgarian Legation.
This untoward occurrence caused unheard-of repercussions,
Giving rise to epidemics of sword-clanking in the Prussians.
The Poles began to threaten, and the Finns began to flap at him,
Directing all the blame for this unfortunate mishap at him;
While the Swedes withdrew entirely from the Anglo-Saxon dailies
The right of photographing the Aurora Borealis,
And, all efforts at rapprochement in the meantime proving barren,
The Japanese in self-defence annexed the Isle of Arran.
My platypus, once thought to be more cautious and more tentative

Than any other living diplomatic representative,
Was now a sort of warning to all diplomatic students
Of the risks attached to negligence, the perils of imprudence,
And, branded in the Honours List as 'Platypus, Dame Vera',
Retired, a lonely figure, to lay eggs in Bordighera.

THE HIPPOPOTAMUS

I had a Hippopotamus, I kept him in a shed
I fed him upon vitamins and vegetable bread
I made him my companion on many cheery walks
And had his portrait done by a celebrity in chalks

His charming eccentricities were known on every side
The creature's popularity was wonderfully wide
He frolicked with the Rector in a dozen friendly tussles
Who could not but remark upon his hippopotamuscles

If he should be afflicted by depression or the dumps
By hippopotameasles or the hippopotamumps
I never knew a particle of peace 'till it was plain
He was hippopotamasticating properly again

I had a Hippopotamus, I loved him as a friend
But beautiful relationships are bound to have an end
Time takes, alas! our joys from us and robs us of our blisses
My hippopotamus turned out a hippopotamisses.

MIA CARLOTTA

Guiseppe, da barber, ees greata for 'mash'
He gotta da bigga, da blacka mustache,
Good clo'es an' good styla an playnta good cash.

W'enevra Guiseppe ees walk on da street,
Da people dey talka, 'How nobby! How neat!
How softa da handa, how smalla da feet'.

He raisa hees hat an' he shaka hees curls,
An' smila weeth teetha so shiny like pearls;
Got many da hearts of da seely young girls.

Carlotta she walka weeth nose in da air,
An' look through Guiseppe weeth far-away stare,
As eef she no see dere ees som'body dere.

Guiseppe, da barber, he gotta da cash.
He gotta da clo'es an' da bigga mustache,
He gotta da seely young girls for da 'mash',
But notta-
You bat my life, notta -
Carlotta,
He gotta!

Thomas Augustine Daly (1871-1948), Irish-American journalist and poet

I vow to thee my country – all earthly things above-
Entire and whole and perfect, the service of my love,
The love that asks no questions; the love that stands the test,
That lays upon the altar the dearest and the best;
The love that never falters, the love that pays the price,
The love that makes undaunted the final sacrifice.

And there's another country I've heard of long ago,
Most dear to them that love her, most great to them that know.
We may not count her armies, we may not see her King;
Her fortress is a faithful heart, her pride is suffering;
And soul by soul and silently her shining bounds increase.
And her ways are ways of gentleness and all her paths are peace.

Sir Cecil Spring-Rice (1859-1918), British ambassador to United States.
Double first at Oxford. Best man to President Roosevelt

A MACHINE

What nudity as beautiful as this
Obedient monster purring at its toil;
Those naked iron muscles dripping oil,
And the sure-fingered rods that never miss?
This long and shining flank of metal is
Magic that greasy labour cannot spoil:
While this vast engine that could rend the soil
Conceals its fury with a gentle hiss.
It does not vent its loathing, it does not turn
Upon its makers with destroying hate.
It bears a deeper malice; lives to earn
Its master's bread and laughs to see this great
Lord of the earth, who rules but cannot learn,
Become a slave of what his slaves create.

Louis Untermeyer (1885-1977), American poet, anthologist, critic and
Marxist. Consultant in Poetry to Library of Congress

THE SYCOPHANTIC FOX AND THE GULLIBLE CROW

A raven sat upon a tree,
And not a word he spoke, for
His beak contained a piece of Brie,
Or, maybe it was Roquefort.
We'll make it any kind you please-
At all events, it was cheese.

Beneath the tree's umbrageous limb
A hungry fox sat smiling;
He saw the raven watching him
 And spoke in words beguiling:
'J'admire,' said he, 'ton beau plumage'.
(Which was simply persiflage.)

'Sweet fowl', he said, 'I understand
You're more than simply natty,
I hear you sing to beat the band
And Adelina Patti.
Pray render with your liquid toungue
A bit from "Gotterdammerung"'.

This subtle speech was aimed to please
The crow and it succeeded;
He thought no bird in all the trees
Could sing as well as he did.
In flattery completely doused
He gave the 'Jewel Song' from 'Faust'.

But gravitation's law, of course,
As Isaac Newton showed it,
Exerted on the cheese its force
And elsewhere soon bestowed it.
In fact, there is no need to tell
What happened when to earth it fell.

I blush to add that when the bird
Took in the situation
He said one brief, emphatic word
Unfit for publication.
The fox was greatly startled, but
He only sighed and answered 'Tut'.

The moral is: a fox is bound
To be a shameless sinner.
But also: when the cheese comes round
You know it's after dinner.
But (what is only known by few)
The fox is after dinner too.

Guy Wetmore (1873-1904), American humorist and poet

ST EUSTON

(By one who is not going)

Stranger with the pile of luggage
Proudly labelled for Portree.
How I wish, this night of August
I were you and you were me.
Think of all that lies before you
When the train goes sliding forthcoming
And the lines athwart at sunset
Lead you swiftly to the North.
Think of breakfast at Kingussie
Think of high Drumochter Pass,
Think of Highland breezes singing
Through the bracken and the grass.
Scabious blue and yellow daisy
Tender fern beside the train.
Rowdy Trummel, falling, brawling
Seen and lost and glimpsed again.
Clachaharry, Achnashellash,
Achnasheen and Duirinish.

Every moor alive with coveys,
Every pool aboil with fish.
Every well remembered vista more
Exciting mile by mile
'Till the wheeling gulls are screaming
Round the engine of The Kyle.
Think of cloud on Beinn na
Cailleach, jagged Cuillins soaring high.
Smell of peat and all the glamour
Of the mighty Isle of Skye.
Rods and guncase in the carriage,
Wise retriever in the van.
Go, and good luck go with you.
(Wish I'd half your luck my man.)

AM Hubbard, author. Circa 1950. The 'Riff' of Riff Raff Authors

---

PARODIES

Parodies occupy a literary niche all of their own and there are anthologies
full of prose and poetry parodied with varying skill. The best are based on
an affection for the original and are often a resource for popular humour:

... The parodists, the pastiche makers,
The copyists, the honest fakers.
We take a published verse and bend
Its purpose to a different end;
We have our sport, but come the day
That minor talent slips away.

Philip Nicholson (1940-2005), novelist, author of the
Creasy thrillers under the pen name AJ Quinnell

Here are two (rather bawdy) parodies of You're the Top! And a neat parody
of Auden's legendary The Night Mail. But first the original:

YOU'RE THE TOP!

You're the top! You're the Coliseum.
You're the top! You're the Louvre museum.
You're the melody from a symphony by Strauss.
You're an Ascot bonnet, a Shakespeare sonnet,
You're Mickey Mouse.

You're the Nile! You're the Tower of Pisa.
You're the smile on the Mona Lisa.
I'm a worthless check, a total wreck, a flop.
But if baby I'm the bottom, you're the top!

You're the top! You're Mahatma Gandhi.
You're the top! You're Napoleon brandy.
You're the purple light of a summer night in Spain.
You're the National Gallery; you're Garbo's salary,
You're cellophane!

You're sublime; you're a turkey dinner.
You're the time of a Derby winner.
I'm a toy balloon that's fated soon to pop;
But if baby I'm the bottom, you're the top!

You're the top! You're a Waldorf salad.
You're the top! You're a Berlin ballad.
You're the nimble tread of the feet of Fred Astaire.
You're an O'Neill drama; you're Whistler's mama;
You're Camembert.

You're a rose; you're Inferno's Dante.
You're the nose on the great Durante.
I'm a lazy lout who is just about to stop,
But if baby I'm the bottom, you're the top!

Cole Porter (1889-1964), American composer and song writer. French Foreign Legionnaire. Gay but happily married. Crippled and leg amputated

YOU'RE THE TOP

You're the top! You're Miss Pinkham's tonic.*
You're the top! You're high colonic.
You're the rhythmic beat of a bridal suite in use.
You're the mound of Venus.
You're King Kong's penis.
You're self-abuse.
You're an arch in the Rome collection.
You're the starch in a groom's erection.
You're the eunuch who
Has just gone through an op.
But if baby you're the bottom, I'm the top!

*Attributed to Sir **Noel** **Pierce** **Coward** (1899-1973), gay playwright,
composer, songwriter, director, actor and singer. Lover, at 14,
of Philip Streatfield. Fellow of Royal Society of Literature.
Friend of Elizabeth, the Queen Mother*

YOU'RE THE TOP

You're the reek of an aging herring.
You're a week spent with Herman Goering.
You're the holy hell of post coital tristesse.
You're a ripe carbuncle. A type of uncle who wears a dress.

You're a shoe that's made by Bally.
You're a sock from Mohammed Ali.
I'm a homeless pet, a New York Met, a flop,
But if baby I'm the bottom, you're the top!

Al Silver

---

*Lydia E Pinkham's Vegetable Compound was marketed by Miss (actually Mrs) Pinkham in
the late 19th century as a 'positive cure for all those painful Complaints and Weaknesses so
common to our female population'. She was a well meaning charlatan who earned a fortune by
acknowledging a monthly biological occurrence and peddling a useless syrup.*

THE NIGHT TRAIN
(after The Night Mail by WH Auden)

This is the Night Train crossing the Border
Air conditioning out of order
Windows sealed, atmosphere muggy
Outside breezy, inside fuggy
Seats for the rich, straps for the poor
Everyone else stuffed up by the door
'We apologise for the sudden halt
We'd like to remind you it's all Railtrack's fault'
This is the Night Train re-crossing the border
Forward lever out of order
'Ladies and Gentlemen, no cause for concern
In eight mile's time we'll attempt to turn
Why not try a microwaved pasty
Or our new Spongiburger, naughty but nasty'
Coffee for the rich, chips for the poor
With a sudden lurch, they're over the floor
Hissing noisily, horribly crammed
Deary me! The sliding door's jammed
This is the Night Train, re-re-crossing the border
Toilets temporarily out of order
Ladies requested to cross their legs
Gentlemen advised to purchase pegs
'Customers requested to remain at ease
If you still fell desperate, cross your knees'
Leaves are busy growing, dreaming of the day
They can fall on the line to cause a delay
Cows staring at passengers all asleep
They think to themselves 'They're just like sheep'
This is the Night Train re-re-crossing the border
Signals and points are out of order
'No time of arrival billed as yet -
Why not try our new filled baguette?'
Groans of defiance, sighs of despair
Hands clenched in anger or pulling out hair

Passengers demanding information
On times of arrival at their destination
Executives bursting with curses and moans
Fishing in pockets for mobiles phones
Calls to the secretary: 'Cancel my meeting'
Calls to the conference: 'Rearrange the seating'
Calls to the PA: 'Reschedule my life!'
Calls to colleagues and calls to the wife,
Calls to the operator: 'I demand compensation!'
Calls to the mistress in a huff at the station.
Moans from the oldies ('Disgraceful innit?')
Threats from the kids ('Stop that this minute!')
Abuse from hooligans, harumphs from commuters
Tapping out grievances on personal computers:
'Never again... prepared to do battle...
Absolute outrage... herded like cattle'
At last! The conductor, braving the squeeze
"When will we get there?' 'Don't ask! Tickets please!'

This is the Night Train, re-re-crossing the border
Overhead lights out of order
Arrival delayed until 12.52
'So why not try our pizza vindaloo?
Or a tasty marsala, buy two get-one-free
Or a piping hot beverage, spilt straight on your knee?'
This is the Night Train re-re-re-re-crossing the border
Whoops! We're off the rails! Apologies in order.
'Owing to derailment, we suggest you alight
And if you run fast, you'll be home by tonight.'

Craig Brown (b 1957), critic, satirist and parodist.
Contributor to Private Eye, parliamentary sketch writer for
The Times. Etonian. Married to Frances Welch

6 | Countryside and Nature

Count no men poor who have the stars above.
The peace and quietude of evening hours
And in their heart that rarest gift of love
And in their garden – flowers.

Evelyn St Leger (1861-1944), author

The first bird I searched for was the nightjar, which used to nest in the valley. Its song is like the sound of a stream of wine spilling from a height into a deep and booming cask. It is an odorous sound, with a bouquet that rises to the quiet sky. In the glare of day it would seem thinner and drier, but dusk mellows it and gives it vintage. If a song could smell, this song would smell of crushed grapes and almonds and oak wood. The sound spills out, and none of it is lost. The whole wood brims with it. Then it stops. Suddenly, unexpectedly. But the ear hears it still, a prolonged and fading echo, draining and winding out among the surrounding trees.

JA Baker (1926-1987). From 'The Peregrine' (winner of the Duff Cooper Memorial Prize), 1967

What a man needs in gardening is a cast iron back with a hinge in it.

Charles Dudley Warner (1829-1900), American essayist and novelist. President of the National Institute of Arts and Letters

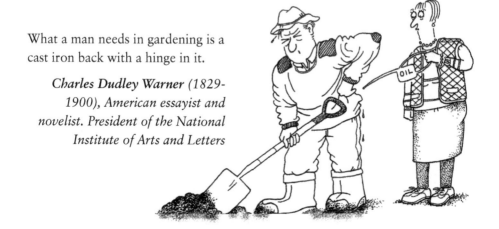

Stationary high pressure has kept the garden in a trance for the last three weeks. Without a breath of wind, a drop of rain or a nip of frost the trees have undressed as quietly as in a bedroom, their leaves falling round them like petticoats to lie in perfect circles at their feet.

This is something I've never seen before: each tree's whole canopy of leaves a distinct disc on the grass. No two discs are exactly the same colour: even of two oaks standing side by side, one's leaves are a darker, rustier brown.

The sorbuses not only have the widest range of colours, but also of leaf textures, from the big round plates of the king of whitebeams, Sorbus mitchellii, yellow one side, grey the other, to the crisp fretwork of S esserteauiana or S calaris (both Szechwanese rowans). As for their palette, no colour seems to be missing except blue.

There is the pinkish plum colour of S vilmorinii, almost matching its faint pink berries, fading to white. Next to it, their garments just overlapping on the ground, S hupehinsis is the mingled yellow, orange and pink of a ripe peach. Before its leaves dropped the tree seemed to be lit from within; a 300-watt bulb at least. Now it stands raw-boned but festooned with ivory berries.

'Joseph Rock's' berries are bright yellow; its puddle a fauve blend of colours: green, plum, brown, splashed with orange and scarlet. The straight trunk of S alnifolia rises from a circle of parchment... and then there are the maples: Norway bright as butter but Caucasian more saturated; less sulphur and more canary. The Japanese maples this year are disappointing, but made up for by the pyrotechnics of Berberis thunbergii and the soldier-red of the chokeberry.

When leaves have fallen on bushes below, or landed on yews or cypresses, there is another new effect: a paint-splatter sometimes almost hiding the ground colour. The huge dirty brown leaves of Populus lasiocarpa smothered a cotoneaster like a nasty accident.

No two autumns are alike. This time horse-chestnuts are like marmalade, spindles like pallid new Beaujolais – and yet some usually reliable fires have not kindled at all.

Hugh Johnson (b 1939), wine expert and gardener. ('Tradescant'). Published in The Garden Magazine, January 1994

In order to live off a garden you have to live in it.

Frank McKinney 'Kin' Hubbard (1868-1930),
American cartoonist, journalist and screenwriter

A robin redbreast in a cage
Should put all heaven in a rage.

William Blake *(1757-1827), poet, engraver, painter*
and printmaker of the Romantic Age

The tree which moves some to tears of joy is in the eyes of others
only a green thing which stands in the way.

ibid

Irish gardens beat all for horror. With nineteen gardeners,
Lord Talbot of Malahide has produced a replica of a suburban
golfcourse.

Nancy Freeman- Mitford *(1904-1973),*
novelist, biographer and journalist

When you get to a certain age, herbaceous
borders hold all the interest

To the endlessly repeated question 'When is your garden at its
best?' one of the commonest replies is 'On the ninth of July'.

*Christopher Lloyd, 'Christo' (1921-2006), author and gardener
at Great Dixter*

Modern fame is nothing. I'd rather have an acre of land.

Lord Tennyson (1809-1892), Poet Laureate

Gardening breaks my nails, my back, my patience and my heart.

*The Hon Victoria Mary 'Vita' Sackville-West (1892-1962), poet,
novelist and garden designer. Chatelaine of Sissinghurst.
Lover of Virginia Woolf and Violet Trefusis*

The year's at the spring
And the day's at the morn;
Morning's at seven;
The hillside's dew-pearled;

The lark's on the wing;
The snail's on the horn
God's in his heaven
All's right with the world.

Robert Browning (1812-1889), Victorian poet

Old Adam was a gardener, and God who made him sees
That half a proper gardener's work is done upon his knees,
So when your work is finished, you can wash your hands and pray
For the Glory of the Garden, that it may not pass away!
And the Glory of the Garden it shall never pass away!

*Rudyard Kipling (1865-1936), poet and novelist.
Declined both Poet Laureate and Knighthood*

Pour faire un jardin, il faut un morceau de terre et l'éternité.

Gilles Clemant (d 1943), French gardener and botanist

A garden is a thing of beauty

... and a job for ever

Every garden, however small, should have a few acres of rough woodland.

Lionel de Rothschild (1882-1941), banker and politician

THE GARDENING DOCTOR

Do you suffer from plumbago?
Is your back a little sore?
Or perhaps it's pyrocanthus
Which you caught in Singapore?
You've a nasty little hosta
Which I think I'll have to lance
And I notice a spirea
Has been leading you a dance!

Are you getting quite forgetful?
Is nemesia the cause?
Does your antirrhinum pain you
When you're walking out of doors?
You've had skimmia rubella,
I can see that by your nose
And cornus capitosa
Has played havoc with your toes!

How is you viburnum tinus?
Have you lost your sense of smell?
Use a syringa reflexa
That should help to keep it well.
I'm afraid your macrocarpus
Isn't really up to scratch
And do avoid nigella
It's a nasty thing to catch!

Still I think you're doing nicely;
Watch the quercus in your knees;
Take your berberis twice nightly.

Next patient please.

Anon

Collective nouns cover very many animals and birds and a few fish. Their origins are often obscure and may sometimes be recorded only as a result of a single mention in the Medieval manuscript The Book of St Albans (1486) (These seem to suggest that the author has probably made them up). There are a number of published books that list hundreds of collective nouns but some that I have come across and find entertaining and often appropriate (ignoring any historical attributes) are:

A Bellowing of Bullfinches

A Chattering of Choughs

A Raft of Coots

A Murder of Crows

A Pitiouness of Doves

A Paddling of Ducks

A Convocation of Eagles

A Trembling of Finches

A Flamboyance of Flamingos

An Omniscience of Godwits

A Confusion of Guineafowl

A Kettle of Hawks

A Troubling of Hummingbirds

A Party of Jays

An Exultation of Larks

A Deceit of Lapwings

A Mischief of Magpies

A Puddling of Mallards

A Parliament of Owls

A Prattle of Parrots

An Ostentation of Peacocks

A Squadron of Pelicans

A Congregation of Plovers

A Conspiracy of Ravens

A Quarrel of Sparrows

A Murmuration of Starlings

A Ballet of Swans

A Herd of Wrens

A Busyness of Ferrets

A Skulk of Foxes

A Husk of Hares

A Labour of Moles

A Bloat of Hippopotomi

A Leap of Leopards

A Crash of Rhinoceros

THE OYSTER

The oyster's a confusing suitor:
It's masc., and fem., and even neuter,
But whether husband, pal or wife
It leads a painless sort of life.
I'd like to be an oyster, say,
In August, June, July and May

Ogden Nash (1902-1971), American humorous poet

THE BLACKBIRD

The nightingale has a lyre of gold,
The lark's is a clarion call,
And the blackbird plays but a boxwood flute,
But I love him best of all.

For his song is all of the joy of life,
And in the mad Spring weather,
We two have listened till he sang
Our hearts and lips together.

*William E Henley (1849-1903), poet, literary critic and editor. Left leg
amputated and he became the inspiration for Long John Silver
in Stevenson's 'Treasure Island'. Daughter Wendy was immortalised
by JM Barrie in 'Peter Pan'. Modelled by Rodin*

... it is wonderful to think
One blackbird can out sing
The voice of all the swarming stars
On any day in Spring

*Harold Monro (1879-1932) poet. Proprietor of The Poetry Bookshop.
"None did more to advance 20th century poetry" (Dominic Hibberd)*

... at the bent sprays' edge
That's the wise thrush; he sings each song twice over
Lest you should think he never could recapture
The first fine careless rapture

*Robert Browning (1812-1889) poet and playwright. Aged fourteen
fluent in French, Greek, Italian and Latin. In Florence, published
The Ring and the Book: 20,000 lines in twelve books. Buried in
Poets Corner, Westminster Abbey beside Tennyson*

7 | Prayers, Religion and Morality

BLESSED MARY, WE BELIEVE
THAT WITHOUT SIN THOU DIDST CONCEIVE.
HOLY VIRGIN, THUS BELIEVING,
MAY WE SIN WITHOUT CONCEIVING?

Edinburgh University

A PRAYER FOR MY GRANDDAUGHTER

Let no one hurry her, Lord.
Give her that rare, that incomparable, gift of time;
Days to dream, dragonfly days when the kingfisher
Suddenly opens for her a window on Wonder.
Let no one worry her, Lord.
Let her wander lark happy through childhood,
By fern curled streams, fringed butter yellow with king cups;
By secret ways that paws have worn through the wild.
Give her cuckoo-loud days and the owl's cry by night.

Dear Lord, give her rainbows.
Show her a west full with sky blue promises;
Scoop up the sounding oceans for her in a shell.
Let her keep her dreams
So that she will always turn her face to the light;
Live merrily, love well;
Hold out ungloved hands for flower and child;
Be easy with animals; come to terms with time.
Lord, let her keep her dreams
Let her riches be remembered, happy days.

Jesus permit thy gracious name to stand
As the first effort of an infant's hand.
And while the fingers on the canvas move
Engage a tender thought to seek thy love
With thy dear children. And let her have a part
And write thy name thyself upon her heart.

Elisabeth White

TOASTS

Sir, A grace used occasionally by the urological surgeons has a certain charm:

We thank thee, O our Lord divine,
Who turned the water into wine,
Take pity on us foolish men,
We're going to turn it back again.

Sir, I thought it might be of interest to readers to hear of the West of Scotland ecumenical grace:

O Lord heap blessings on the soup, heap blessings on the stovies,
Heap blessings on the Papes and Jews, the Muslims and Jehovies.
Heap blessings on all gathered here, on absent friends and strangers,
And if you have any blessings left, for God's sake bless the Rangers.

Sir, A grace I have used on occasion may strike a chord with some of your readers:

Be present at our table, Lord,
With guests we must, but can't afford,
Help us betray no sign of fuss,
As if we've always feasted thus;
And make the daily lady stay
Till half past ten to clear away.

Sir Archibald Birkmyre (1875-1935), Scottish jute manufacturer in India.
From The Times

From the inability to let well alone; from too much zeal for the new and contempt for what is old; from putting knowledge before wisdom, science before art, and cleverness before common sense; from treating patients as cases, and from making the cure of the disease more grievous than its endurance, Good Lord deliver us.

Sir Robert Hutchison (d 1960), Scottish physician

You that have faith to look with fearless eyes
Beyond the tragedy of a world at strife
And trust that out of might and death shall rise
The dawn of ampler life.
Rejoice whatever anguish rend your heart
That God has given you as his priceless dower
To live and play your part
In freedom's crowning hour.

Wilfred Owen (1983-1918), poet and soldier

ABOU BEN ADHEM

Abou Ben Adhem (may his tribe increase!)
Awoke one night from a deep dream of peace,
And saw, within the moonlight in his room,
Making it rich, and like a flower in bloom,
An angel writing in a book of gold.
Exceeding peace had made Ben Adhem bold,
And to the presence in the room he said,
'What writest thou?' – The vision rais'd its head,
And with a look made of all sweet accord,
Answer'd, 'The names of those who love the Lord.'
'And is mine one?' said Abou. 'Nay, not so,'
Replied the angel. Abou spoke more low,
But cheerly still; and said, 'I pray thee, then,
Write me as one that loves his fellow men.'

The angel wrote, and vanish'd. The next night
It came again with a great wakening light,
And show'd the names whom love of God had blest,
And lo! Bed Adhem's name led all the rest.

Leigh Hunt (1784-1859), critic, poet and writer. Friend of Keats and
Shelley. Based on a story in Bibliotheque Orientale about a Persian sufi

I recollect once seeing God in a dream far above in the most distant firmament. He was looking contentedly out of a little window in the sky, a devout, hoary-headed being with a small Jewish beard, and he was scattering forth myriads of seed-corns, which, as they fell from heaven, burst open in the infinitude of space, and expanded to vast dimensions till they became actual, radiant, blossoming, peopled worlds, each one as large as our own globe.

Heinrich Heine (1797-1856), German poet and literary critic

Saint Peter sat by the celestial gate:
His keys were rusty, and the lock was dull,
So little trouble had been given of late;
Not that the place by any means was full,
The angels were singing out of tune,
And hoarse with having little else to do,
Excepting to wind up the sun and moon,
Or curb a runaway young star or two,
Or wild colt of a comet, which too soon
Broke out of bounds o'er the ethereal blue.
Splitting some planet with its playful tail,
As boats are sometimes by a wanton whale.

Lord George Gordon Byron (1788-1824), Romantic poet,
from 'The Vision of Judgement', 1822

Wherever God erects a house of prayer, the devil builds a chapel there and commands the largest congregation.

Daniel Defoe (born Daniel Foe) (1660-1731), wool merchant,
writer and journalist. 500 books and pamphlets.

ON PSALM CXXXVI

Let us with a gladsome mind
Praise the Lord for he is kind;
For his mercies aye endure,
Ever faithful, ever sure.

[*And forty four more lines until...*]

Let us, therefore, warble forth
His mighty majesty and worth,
That his mansion hath on high,
Above the reach of mortal eye.

John Milton (1608-1674), poet, author, tutor, civil servant and
statesman. Fluent in six languages including Old English.
Married three times. Written at the age of 12 in 1620

For each child thou shalt plant a tree,
That the womb of thy Earthly Mother
Shall bring forth life,
As the womb of woman doth bring forth life.
He who doth destroy a tree
Hath cut off his own limbs.

All men will become brothers once again
Under thy spreading branches,
As the Heavenly Father hath loved all his children,
So shall we love and care for the trees
That grow in our land,
So shall we keep and protect them,
That they may grow tall and strong,
And fill the earth again with their beauty.
For the trees are our Brothers,
And as Brothers,
We shall guard and love one another.

Extract from 'The Essene Teachings of the Dead Sea Scrolls', translated
*from the original Hebrew and Aramaic text by **Edmund Bordeaux Szekely***
(1905-1979), Hungarian linguist, philosopher and psychologist

Soto tu abiria dereva Mungu.
[We are all passengers, God is the driver.]

Swahili saying

There is always music amongst the trees but our hearts must
be very still to hear it.

*Minnie Aumonier, poet and painter. Believed to be
from 'Gardens in the Sun and Shade', 1920*

Almighty Father, thy love is like a great sea that girdles the earth. Out of the
deep we come to float awhile upon its surface. We cannot sound its depth
nor tell its greatness only we know it never faileth. The winds that blow
over us are the breathing of thy spirit; the sun that lights and warms us is
thy truth. Now thou does suffer us to sail calm seas; now thou dost buffet us
with the storms of trouble; on the crest of waves of sorrow thou dost raise us
but it is thy love that bears us up; in the trough of desolation thou dost sink
us that we may see nought but they love on every side. And when we pass
into the deep again, the waters of love encompass and enfold us. The foolish
call them the waters of misery but those who have heard the whisper of thy
spirit know them for the boundless ocean of eternal life and love.

Anonymous

Sir,

I have come across some prayerful prayers for our time, constructed in
the style of The Lord's Prayer but not I trust offensive. The Lord's Prayer
after all has been an endlessly useful vehicle for verse and I can still recall
the old London omnibus conductor's version which begins: 'Our Father
which art in Hendon, Harrow Road be they name. Thy Kingston Common,
thy Wimbledon... etc. This new version is a little less jolly, the hardness
deriving from our present plight. It is called The British Prayer:

> Our Father which art in Downing Street
> Harold be thy name.
> United Kingdom gone,

We shall be done on earth and probably in heaven.
Give us each day our dearer bread,
And forgive us our devaluations
As we forgive them that speculate against us.
Lead us not into the Common Market
But deliver us to the unions.
For this is the kingdom, no power, no Tory.
For ever and ever, Amen

Letter to The Financial Times. Harold Wilson was Prime Minister
1964-1970 and 1974-1976

A PRAYER FOR TOURISTS

Heavenly Father, look down on us your humble, obedient tourist servants who are doomed to travel this earth, taking photographs, sending postcards and buying souvenirs. We beseech you, O Lord, to see our plane is not hijacked, our luggage is not lost and our overweight baggage goes unnoticed. Give us this day divine guidance in our selection of hotels. We pray that the telephones work and that the operators speak our language.

Lead us to good, inexpensive restaurants where the wine is included in the price of the meal. Give us the wisdom to tip correctly in currencies we do not understand. Make the natives love us for what we are and not for what we can contribute to their worldly goods. Grant us the strength to visit museums, cathedrals, palaces and if we skip a few historic monuments to take a nap after lunch, have mercy for our flesh is weak.

Dear God, protect our wives from 'bargains' they don't need or can't afford. Lead them not into temptation for they know not what they do.

Almighty Father, keep our husbands from looking at foreign women and comparing them with us. Save them from making fools of themselves in nightclubs. Above all please do not forgive them their trespasses for they know exactly what they do.

And then, when our voyage is over, grant us the favour of finding someone who will look at our holiday snaps and listen to our stories, so that our lives as tourists will not have been in vain. Amen.

Art Buchwald (1925-2007), American humorist, best known
for a column in The Washington Post that ran for 27 years

A PRAYER FOR GARDENERS

Oh Lord, grant that in some way it may rain every day from about midnight until three o'clock in the morning, but you see, it must be gentle and warm so that it can soak in; grant that at the same time it would not rain on the campium, alyssum, helianthemum, lavender and the others which you, in your infinite wisdom, know are drought loving plants; and grant that the sun may shine all day long, but not everywhere (not, for instance on spirea, or on gentian, plantain lily and rhododendron) and not too much; that there may be plenty of dew and little wind, enough for worms, no plant lice or snails and no mildew; and that once a week a thin liquid manure may fall from heaven. For so it was in the Garden of Eden, otherwise things would not have grown as well as you say that they did.

Karel Capek (1890-1938) Czech writer, dramatist, gardener, publisher,
literary and art critic

A PRAYER FOR SECRETARIES

Dear Lord, help me to do my work well; to have the memory of an elephant; the patience of a saint; and the hide of a rhinoceros.

And when the boss asks me to stay late to type a three page letter that absolutely must go out today and then he doesn't sign it until tomorrow, please help me to keep my mouth shut.

Dear Lord, never let me lose patience, even when the boss has me searching the files for hours for something that is later discovered on his desk.

Help me to have the knowledge of a genius although my education is limited to high school and secretarial training.

Let me always know exactly where my boss is and when he will be back, even though he never tells me either.

Help me to understand and carry out all instructions without any explanation.

And Lord, when the year ends and when I am told emphatically 'Destroy these files', give me the foresight to keep those that will be asked for in a few days.

Let the great shepherd lead:
and by winding ways, not without pastures and still waters,
we shall climb insensibly and reach the tops of the everlasting hills,
where the winds are cool and the sight is glorious

Inscription on a memorial by the road leading to Loch an Eilean,
Badenoch and Strathspey, Invernesshire

Of course God will forgive me. That's his job.

Heinrich Heine *(1797-1856), German journalist and literary critic*

Make us not like porridge, stiff and stodgy, but more like
cornflakes – crisp and ready to serve.

Bishop of Swansea and Brecon, 1980

AN IRISH PRAYER

May God give you
For every storm a rainbow,
For every tear, a smile.
For every care, a promise
And a blessing for each trial.
For every problem sent in life
A faithful friend to share.
For every sigh, a sweet song
And an answer for each prayer.

Go to Heaven for the climate, go to Hell for the people.

Mark Twain *(Samuel Langhorne Clemens) (1835-1910),*
American author and humorist

8 | Miscellaneous

VILLAGE NAMES

Our Anglo-Saxon heritage, a touch of Huguenot influence, a thousand years of shifting land use, and bowdlerisation have produced some wonderfully appealing local names:

Cambridgeshire..........	Gamlingay Cinques
Cardiff	Splott
Cornwall..............	Praze-an-Beeble
County Durham	Binchester Blocks
	Muggleswick
Derbyshire	Knockerdown

	Upton Snodsbury
Yorkshire	Ainderby Quernhow
(North and South)	Blubberhouses
	Cridling Stubbs
	Glen Hoddle
	Nether Poppleton
	Pisser Clough
	Potto
	Ugglebarnby
	Wet Rain
	Wetwang
Scotland	Arpafeelie (Ross & Cromarty)
	Auchenshuggle (Glasgow)
	Brokenwind (Aberdeen)
	Rest and be Thankfull (Argyll)
	Spunkie (Ayrshire)

A cast of actors from Dorset and Wiltshire?

Carton Denham
Charlton Horethorne
Hardington Mandeville
Wynford Eagle

A repertory company from Grimpo in Shropshire?

Ashford Bowdler
Hope Bowdler
Edwyn Ralph
Aston Munslow
Neen Savage
Maund Bryan
Preston Brockhurst

On a signpost in Lincolnshire that points to Mavis Enderby and Old Bolingbroke somebody has added:

- A GIFT OF A SON

The English inability or obstinacy in pronouncing foreign words is revealed in the names of some of the country's oldest families; themselves often originally refugees from persecution abroad.

As written	As pronounced
Auchinlech	Afflek
Beauchamp	Beacham
Beaulieu	Bewley
Belvoir	Beaver
Caius	Keeys
Cholmondley	Chumley
Cockburn	Coburn
Colquhoun	Cahoon
Featherstonehaugh	Fanshaw
Marjoribanks	Marshbanks
Menzies	Mingiz
Theobald	Tibbald
Tyrwhitt	Tirit
Wymondham	Windam

BOTH IS RIGHT

Passing Bouth in the Southern Lakes, a bus passenger asked if it was pronounced 'Bowth'; 'Yes' said one, but another said it was 'Booth'. Actually, said the driver, it's 'Both'.

Letter to The Guardian, February 2015

During the 1948 war in Palestine, the US Ambassador to the United Nations, Warren Austin, hoped that the Jews and the Arabs would settle their differences: 'Like good Christians'.

SMALL MEDIUM AT LARGE

Sign outside the gypsy caravan of Lou Conran

Field officers must not wear spurs when taking passage in captive balloons.

King's Regulations, early nineteenth century

First bridge player: 'Well, how would you have played that hand?'
Second bridge player: 'Under an assumed name.'

Anon

There has been a run of car-stickers since the late 1970s promoting various sporting and other organisations. Among them:

Hang-gliders do it quietly.
Windsurfers do it standing up.
Waterskiers do it in rubber suits.
Squash players do it against the wall.
Skiers do it on the piste.
Swimmers do it with the breast stroke.
Anaesthetists do it with a general.

There was also the ad slogan 'You can do it in an MG' *and the Qantas car sticker* 'Do it Down Under'.

Inevitably, graffiti variants were soon to hand, promoting little more than double entendres:

> Shot putters do it on one leg.
> Tommy Cooper does it just like that.
> Monks do it habitually.
> Musicians do it by the score.
> Broadcasters do it with frequency.
> Philosophers do it thoughtfully.
> Bankers do it with interest.
> Teachers do it with class.
> Debaters do it orally.
> Tennis players do it with luv.
> Kamikaze pilots do it once.

There are many more.

DOROTHY PARKER

She gave him her nickel with the manner of one presenting a park to a city.

Brevity is the redemption of lingerie.

Tell him I was fucking busy. Or the other way round.

If all the girls were laid end to end, I would not be surprised.
(On attending a dance at Yale)

Excuse my dust
(Her own epitaph)

Dorothy Parker *(1863-1967), American poet, critic and satirist*

Noel Coward watched the Coronation on TV in New York. When the carriage bearing Queen Salote of Tonga came into view a friend asked, 'Who's the fellow sitting with her?' Coward replied: 'Her lunch.' In fact, he was the Sultan of Kelantan.

Jack Benny, to the robber who demanded 'Your money or your life!': 'I'm thinking it over.'

Jack Benny *(1894-1974), American comedian, film actor and violinist*

Playing bridge is like making love. Either you need a terrific partner or a really good hand.

Omar Sharif *(born Michel Dimitri Chaloub) (1932-2015), Egyptian actor and world class bridge player. Fluent in six languages*

Serious sport has nothing to do with fair play. It is bound up with hatred, jealousy, boastfulness and disregard of all the rules.

George Orwell *(1903-1950), novelist, journalist and critic*

Round dowel rods will be used for buttock fouls in sit-down competitions.

Article XII, Section A of the Rules and Regulations of the American Armsport Association (the governing body for competitive arm wrestling)

It's just a job. Grass grows, birds fly, waves pound the sand. I beat people up.

Muhammad Ali *(born Cassius Marcellus Clay) (b 1942), American professional boxer – 56 wins (37 knockouts), 5 losses. Conscientious objector. Four wives, eleven children*

Sir Thomas Beecham (1879-1961), conductor and impresario, was travelling in the no-smoking carriage of a train. A woman passenger lit a cigarette with the words, 'You won't object if I smoke?' To which Beecham replied, 'Certainly not – and you won't object if I'm sick.' It was in the days when the railways were still privately owned. 'I don't think you know who I am,' the woman angrily pointed out, 'I am one of the directors' wives.' To which Beecham riposted, 'Madam, if you were the director's only wife, I should still be sick.'

SNEEZING

Increasingly, even among English speakers the German 'Gesundheit!' is heard. In France, some say an explosive 'A tes souhaits!' for the same effect, while, among Spanish speakers it could be 'Jesus!', or 'Salud!'. In Korea, I believe, they say 'Sai eichi!' and many Slavic speakers (including Poles and Russians) may say 'Nazdorovie!'. Few such expressions are religious, but all echo the distinctive sound and they convey regards for good health. Correspondence in The Times culminated in this comprehensive letter:

Sir, English people and Americans say 'Bless you'. Germans say 'Gesundheit' ('health') or 'Gescheitheit' ('cleverness!'). Likewise the Dutch say 'Gezondheid'. Lithuanians say 'I sveikata' ('to your health!'). Iranians say 'Afiyat bashe' ('I wish you good health'). The French say 'A tes souhaits' ('may your wishes come true') or 'A tes amours' ('to your loves!'). Spanish and Mexicans say 'Salud!' ('health!') for one sneeze and 'Salud y dinero!' ('health and money') for two. The Japanese say 'Ichi home' ('praise') for one sneeze, 'Ni-kusashi' ('criticism') for two, 'San-kenashi' ('disparagement') for three and 'Yottsu-ijo wa kaze no moto' ('sign of a cold coming!') for more.'

October 2004

'Nah chee dah' (Burmese, literally 'your nose is running').

Reddy, 29, MBA, (Russia), Uttra, V Fair, Slim, clean habits owns fairly decent assets in Chennai from a well settled business family engaged in business. Seeks Graduate Reddy girl from well settled Telugu family. Preferably home maker. But not a must. Please contact with horoscope details. Cell 0-944443-91787.

Advertisement in Kathmandu Post, 2 September 2007

We open most days about 9 or 10. Occasionally as early as 7 but on some days as late as 12 or even 1. We close about 5.30 or 6. Occasionally about 4 or 5 but sometimes as late as 11 or 12.

On some days or afternoons we are not here at all. Lately, we've been here just about all the time, except when we're somewhere else – but we should be here then too.

Shop window notice, County Antrim

The comfort of the rich depends on an abundant supply of the poor.

Francois-Marie Arouet Voltaire (1694-1778), French historian, philosopher and playwright

Following a bout of hepatitis, Frank Muir had one testicle removed. Accused in a BBC word game of being diabolical, he replied 'I am monobolical'.

Frank Muir (1929-1998), comedy writer and raconteur. "Educated in E10"

Emperor Gordian, 159-238. Emperor for 36 days.
His manners were less pure, but his character was equally amiable with that of his father. Twenty-two acknowledged concubines and a library of sixty-two thousand volumes, attested to the variety of his inclinations and from the productions which he left behind him, it appears that the former as well as the latter were designed for use rather than ostentation.

Edward Gibbon (1737-1794), MP, historian

The following four entries have been lifted from 'Lists of Note', compiled by Shaun Usher and published by Unbound in 2013.

WARTIME RULES OF RICHMOND GOLF COURSE, 1940

Players are asked to collect Bomb and Shrapnel splinters to save these causing damage to the Mowing Machines.

In Competitions, during gunfire or while bombs are falling, players may take cover without penalty for ceasing play.

The positions of known delayed action bombs are marked by red flags placed at a reasonably, but not guaranteed, safe distance therefrom.

Shrapnel and/or bomb splinters on the Fairways, or in Bunkers within a club's length of a ball, may be moved without penalty, and no penalty shall be incurred if a ball is thereby caused to move accidentally.

A ball moved by enemy action may be replaced, or if lost or destroyed, a ball may be dropped not nearer the hole without penalty.

A ball lying in a crater may be lifted and dropped not nearer the hole, preserving the line to the hole, without penalty.

A player whose stroke is affected by the simultaneous explosion of a bomb may play another ball from the same place. Penalty one stroke.

These names were put forward in 1937 for the dwarfs in the Disney film 'Snow White':

Awful	Dizzy	Hotsy	Snappy
<u>Bashful</u>	Doleful	Hungry	<u>Sneezy</u>
Biggo-Ego	Dumpy	Jaunty	Sneezy-Wheezy
Biggy	Flabby	Jumpy	Snoopy
Biggy-Wiggy	Gabby	Lazy	Soulful
Blabby	Gaspy	Neurtsy	Strutty
Busy	Gloomy	Nifty	Tearful
Chesty	Goopy	Puffy	Thrifty
Crabby	Graveful	Sappy	Weepy
Cranky	<u>Grumpy</u>	Scrappy	Wistful
Duffy	<u>Happy</u>	Shifty	Woeful
Dippy	Helpful	Silly	
Dirty	Hoppy	<u>Sleepy</u>	

The chosen names are underlined. Dopey and Doc were chosen later.

Rodney	Rudolph	Roland	Romeo
Roddy	Rudy	Reggy	
Roderick	Rollo	Reginald	

In Italo Calvino's book of 1979, "If on a Winter's Night a Traveler", there is a list of excuses for not buying books.

the Books You Needn't Read;

the Books Made For Purposes Other Than Reading;

the Books That If You Had More Than One Life You Would Certainly Also Read But Unfortunately Your Days Are Numbered;

the Books You Mean To Read But There Are Others You Must Read First;

the Books Too Expensive Now And You'll Wait Till They're Remaindered;

the Books ditto When They Come Out In Paperback;

Books You Can Borrow From Somebody;

Books That Everybody's Read So It's As If You Had Read Them Too;

And a list of reasons for buying books:

the Books You've Been Planning to Read for Ages;

the Books You've Been Hunting for Years Without Success;

the Books Dealing with Something You're Working On At The Moment;

the Books You Want to Own So They'll Be Handy Just In Case;

the Books You Could Put Aside Maybe To Read This Summer;

the Books You Need To Go With Other Books On Your Shelves;

the Books That Fill You With Sudden, Inexplicable Curiosity, Not Easily Justified;

the Books Read Long Ago Which It's Now Time To Reread;

the Books You've Always Pretended To Have Read And Now It's Time To Sit Down And Really Read Them;

the New Books Whose Author Or Subject Appeals To You;

the New Books By Authors Or On Subjects Not New (for you or in general);

New Books By Authors Or On Subjects Completely Unknown (at least to you);

Books You Haven't Read.

Italo Calvino (1923-1985), Italian journalist, agronomist, novelist, one time communist. Most translated of all Itlian writers

He what's takes what isn't isn,
When he gets catched, he goes to prison.

Pam Ayres (b 1947), poet, comedienne, songwriter and presenter.
Advice from her father

It's ten minutes walk – if you run.

Ibid.

A cap of good acid costs $5 and for that you can hear the universal symphony with God singing solo and the Holy Ghost on the drums.

Hunter S Thompson (1937-2005), surrealist painter,
journalist and Hell's Angel

I have a big fire in my soul but no one comes to feel its warmth.

Vincent Van Gogh (1853-1890), Dutch Post-Impressionist painter

She was so poor she hardly knew where the next bottle of champagne was coming from.

*Of **Isadora Duncan** (1877-1927), bisexual American dancer*
who flouted traditional mores and morality

Him I love because he is devoid of fear, carries himself like a man and has a heart as big as his boots. I fancy too that he knows how to enjoy the blessings of life.

Rudyard Kipling describing the kind of man who gets to California.
Indian newspaper 'Pioneer', 12 December 1889

If you can fake sincerity, you can fake anything.

Lawrence Olivier (1907-1989), actor, producer and film director

Reason is and should be the slave of passion.

David Hughes (b 1952), English satirical artist

Dancers are the acrobats of God.

Martha Graham (1894-1991), contemporary dancer and choreographer

Stand up and keep your back straight – that's where your wings will grow.

Ibid

Sir, The idea of pets replacing husbands is not new. When asked why she never married, the novelist Marie Corelli was said to have replied that she had three pets who took the place of a man – a dog that growled all morning, a parrot that swore all evening and a cat that stayed out all night.

Letter to The Times, 1 February 1997

The calm decay of nature, when the mind
retains its strength.

Robert Southey (1774-1843), Romantic poet, from 'Occasional Pieces'

It is not pie in the sky when we die that I want, it's ham, where I am.

African-American preacher, north Florida, February 1990

Lord Finchley tried to mend the electric light
Himself; it struck him dead and serve him right.
It is the duty of a wealthy man
To give employment to the artisan.

Hilaire Belloc (1870-1953), Anglo-French writer and historian.
President of Oxford Union

ROAD SIGNS

Signs, spaced at two-mile intervals, beside a turnpike in Florida:

DON'T LOSE YOUR HEAD TO GAIN A MINUTE
YOU NEED YOUR HEAD, YOUR BRAINS ARE IN IT

DROVE TOO LONG, DRIVER SNOOZING
WHAT HAPPENED NEXT IS NOT AMUSING

Driving through the Indian Himalayas you will see:

DRIVING IS RISKY AFTER WHISKY

BE GENTLE ON MY CURVES

STOP GOSSIPING AND LET HIM DRIVE

To be decadent you first have to civilised.

> *Oscar Wilde (1854-1900), Irish playwright, novelist and poet*

Never ask a man whether he comes from Yorkshire. If he does he will already have told you. If he doesn't, don't humiliate him.

> *Sir Roy Hattersley (b 1932), politician, author and journalist*

England 283, Hutton ill. Sorry, Hutton 111.

> *John Arlott (1914-1991), BBC cricket commentator*

Following lengthy correspondence in The Times on the correct way to serve haggis, the headmaster of Clifton wrote:

There is only one way to serve haggis: slow, left arm and round the wicket.

The bowler's Holding, the batsman's Willey.

Brian Johnston (1912-1994), BBC cricket commentator,
author, and television presenter

Bert Ironmonger was an Australian cricketer who played in the 1930s and
was known for his hopeless batting abilities. On one occasion his wife
telephoned the dressing room and was told that Bert had just gone out to
bat. She replied: "I'll hold."

A brown condom full of walnuts.

Clive James (born Vivian Leopold James), (b 1939), Australian poet,
translator, author, critic and broadcaster, on Arnold Schwarzenegger, five
times Mr Universe. From 'Flying Visits – Postcard from Los Angeles', 1984

Moses, negotiating with God over Commandments, came back
with results. 'There's good news and bad news. Good news –
I've got them down to ten. Bad news – Adultery is in.'

John Pike, Bishop of Sherborne during a sermon, 1902

Sir, Mrs Thatcher is quite right to condemn the unhygienic custom of baby
handling by electioneering parliamentary candidates. My son was sitting in
his perambulator, harmlessly surveying the sea at Criccieth, when he was
patted on the head by Mr Lloyd George. He was bald before he was 30.

Letter to the Daily Telegraph, 20th April 1979

There is nothing more dreadful than imagination without taste.

Johann Wolfgang Goethe (1749-1832), German statesman,
writer and poet

Queen Mary to small boy, 'And where do you live?'
'On Bayswater, Ma'am – op'sit Whiteleys.'
Queen Mary, 'That's nice. I live in Victoria, behind Gorringes.'

Victoria Mary Augusta Louise Olga Pauline Claudine Agnes,
(1867-1953), Queen Consort and wife of King George V. Whiteleys
department store on Bayswater Road was opened in 1860, Gorringes
department store on Buckingham Palace Road closed in 1960s

Neither a wise man nor a brave man lies down on the track
of history to wait for the train of the future to run him over.

Dwight Eisenhower (1890-1969), US President and
Supreme Commander, Allied Forces Europe, 1944

If you cannot comfort the afflicted, afflict the comfortable.

John Kenneth Galbraith (1908-2006), Canadian economist and diplomat

In the margin of a Foreign Office memo was the discreet comment:
Round objects
Lord Halifax sent back the memo with the additional words:
Who is Round, and why does he object?

There's less in this than meets the eye.

Tallulah Bankhead (1902-1968), American actress and reputed
libertine, after seeing a bad play

Everything is at sea, except the fleet.

Sir Horace Walpole (1717-1797), politician and antiquarian

The wisest prophets make sure of the events first.

Anon

The sad lady looked at her whiting with very nearly the same expression as the whiting looked at her.

Georges Simenon (1903-1989), Belgian writer (500 novels) and creator of the detective Jules Maigret. From 'Great French Detective Stories'

Don't be cruel to a vegetable
Remember that a lettuce has a heart
Don't split peas just to please your tongue
And remember when you eat a brussel sprout
You'll be robbing a cabbage of its young.

Denis Norden *(b 1922), comedy writer and television presenter.*
From 'My Music', June 1983

BEECHAM QUOTES

The English may not love music, but they absolutely love the noise it makes.

On hearing an avant-garde composer:
Your music will be remembered long after the music of Beethoven and Bach is forgotten – and not before.

Asked whether he approved of lady instrumentalists he replied:
No. If they are attractive it will upset my players; if the are unattractive, it will upset me".

On being asked if he had ever conducted Stockhausen:
No, but I may have trodden in it.

Sir Thomas Beecham (1879-1961), conductor and impresario.
Founder of London Philharmonic and promoter of opera

Tu m'as rendu fades tous les hommes, et médiocres tous les destins.
[You have made all other men seem insipid, all other destinies mediocre.]

Henri de Montherlant (b 1895), novelist and dramatist.
Quoted by Elisabeth Maxwell, about her husband Robert Maxwell,
Czechoslovakian media mogul and MP, November 1991

I lost two toes in the Mount Cook snows,
And an eye in the Tasman Sea
A hand and a jaw in a circular saw
And a limb in a falling tree.
But the pangs untold of a cough or a cold
I know I need never endure,
If I moisten my throttle in time from a bottle
Of Wood's Great Peppermint Cure.

Advertisement in a New Zealand newspaper

Capricorn Dec 22 – Jan 19: Diversify, highlight versatility, be in touch with recalcitrant relative. Remember: 'Pride goes before a fall'. Gift received adds to wardrobe: people say, 'You look spiffy!'

Bangkok Post, 23 March 1998

Monogamy is OK in the office, but at home I prefer white.

Samuel Goldwyn *(born Szmuel Gelbfisz) (1879-1974). Polish-American film producer. Brother-in-law of Cecil B DeMille*

Monogamy is something you make furniture from.

Ibid

An astronaut and a Christian brain surgeon, both Russian, were discussing religion.
Astronaut: I've been out in space many times, but I've never seen God or angels.
Brain surgeon: I've operated on many clever brains, but I've never seen a single thought.

The girl was beheaded, chopped into pieces and placed in a trunk but was not interfered with.

From a Fleet Street report

What has one wheel and flies? A wheelbarrow full of manure.

John Piper (1903-1992), painter, printer and stained glass designer

What is funny about legs? The bottom is at the top.

From a lady of 92

'I'm afraid', said a woman on entering a shoe shop, 'that one of my feet is larger than the other.' 'Oh no, madam,' exclaimed the salesman, 'if anything one is smaller.'

Exclusive universal tailors

Advertisement

Sole joint agents

Sign outside a house

Bric-à-brac bought / Antiques sold

Notice inside a West Country shop

The reason we can sell our antiques for less is because we buy them direct from the manufacturer

Advertisement in the Washington Star

A mother whale's advice to her young:
Beware, my dears, it is when you are spouting that you are most likely to be harpooned.

What the brassière said to the top hat: 'You go on ahead while I give these two a lift.'

Dame Freya Stark (1893-1993), explorer and travel writer.
Told to the ambassador in Cairo in 1942. It shocked him.

It is possible to be born an aristocrat without ever becoming a gentleman.

Sir Nicholas Ridley (1929-1993), politician, commenting on Germans and Italians. From 'Le Monde'. Grandson of Sir Edwin Lutyens

Thrift is what you do to yourself; meanness is what you do to others.

Anon

Arguing with a woman is like trying to fold the airmail edition of The Times in a high wind.

Lord Mancroft (b 1957), financier and politician

If you are tired of sin, come in. If not, ring...

Notice pinned to the outside of a Liverpool church

Beware of loose women in tight skirts and tight women in loose skirts.

Anon

Flattery is alright if you don't inhale.

Adlai Stevenson (1835-1914), American politician and diplomat.
Vice President (1893-1997)

I have a simple philosophy. Fill what's empty, empty what's full, and scratch where it itches.

Alice Roosevelt Longworth (1884-1980), writer and socialite.
Daughter of President Theodore Roosevelt

Life is what happens while you are making other plans.

John Lennon (1940-1980), singer-songwriter with The Beatles

Woman was made after man, and man has been after her ever since.

Anon

Worcester, like most colleges, does not admit dogs. The Dean's dog Flint has thus officially been declared a cat by the Governing Body.

From the Oxford magazine Isis

George Burns (1896-1996) was asked at the age of 93 what sex was like. He replied:

Like playing billiards with a rope.

DUE TO STAFF SHORTAGE THE AUTOMATIC TICKET MACHINES ARE NOT IN USE.

Notice at Farringdon Underground station

Princess Margaret's lady-in-waiting opened a wedding present for her. It turned out to be a wooden salad server. Carved along its extended handle were the words:

May your Life be one long Spoon.

Sir Osbert Lancaster (1908-1986), cartoonist and stage designer. Fourth class degree (on second taking) from Oxford

It is rarely possible to carry the torch of truth through a crowd without singeing somebody's beard.

Joshua Bruyn (1923-2011), Dutch art historian

I hope I may die before you, so that I may see Heaven before you improve it.

A remark made to Lancelot 'Capability' Brown (1716-1783), landscape architect

Professional men, they have no cares;
Whatever happens, they get theirs

Ogden Nash (1902-1971), American poet and lyricist

A mutilated stump that bled from every vein.

Stefan Zweig on Vienna after WWI

In a British courtroom, an ordinary act like eating a sausage can be made under cross-examination to sound like some bizarre perversion.

Auberon Waugh (1939-2001), journalist. Eldest son of Evelyn Waugh

A radio conversation released by the Chief of US Naval Operations, October 1995:
Canadians: Please divert your course 15 degrees south to avoid a collision.
Americans: Recommend you divert your course 15 degrees north to avoid a collision.
Canadians: Negative. You will have to divert your course 15 degrees to the south to avoid a collision.
Americans: This is the captain of a US Navy ship. I say again, divert your course.
Canadians: No, I say again, you divert your course.
Americans: Now hear this. I am in command of the aircraft carrier USS Lincoln, the largest ship in the United States' Atlantic Fleet. We are accompanied by a task force of three destroyers, three cruisers, and numerous support vessels. I demand that you change your course 15 degrees north. I say again, that is one-five degrees north, or counter-measures will be undertaken to ensure the safety of this ship.
Canadians: This is a lighthouse. Your call.

AJP Taylor as drawn by the cartoonist Mark Boxer, aka Marc: 'He resembled a small creature of the field who was apprehensive of attack but would turn nasty in that event'.

Alan Watkins (1933-2010), political columnist

Start the day with a smile and get it over with.

WC Fields (1880-1946),
American comedian and entertainer

A competition in The Times, some time ago, asked for the unkindest advice to give to a tourist. The winning advice was:

It is customary when using any form of public transport to shake hands with other passengers before disembarking, and to thank them for sharing the journey.

The gimlet-eyed lady was fearless, formidable, eccentric, upper-class and athletic. She had a ten-acre voice.

John le Carré (born David John Moore Cornwell) (b 1931), author, scriptwriter. Goethe Prize winner. From 'Sarratt and the Draper of Watford', 1999

Incest is *relatively* boring. Necrophilia is *dead* boring.

Ogden Nash (1902-1971), American humorist poet and lyricist

It's a small world – and if it isn't you're at the wrong party.

Midwife – The one between two divorces.

Ladies: United you Stand – Divided you Fall.

First bra advert. New York, circa 1922

First date – sofa so good!

A father's advice to his daughter

An atheist is a man who has no invisible means of support.

John Buchan, Lord Tweedsmuir (1875-1940), Scottish novelist and historian. Governor General of Canada

True believers will lie on green grass with young virgins whose breasts are like ripe pomegranates.

The Koran

In 1980 the Marchioness of Dufferin and Ava dismissed a butler over an issue concerning crab apples. He took her to an industrial tribunal. Her old friend Lord Longford offered to speak on her behalf but she assured him 'No thank you, I am in quite enough trouble as it is'.

Maureen Dufferin (1907-1998). One of the 'Guinness Girls' and famous for her forthright manner. Married three times and nicknamed Teapot.

'Bishop, what do you do in your spare time?'
'When I have nothing on I like to curl up on the sofa with my favourite Trollope.'

Edward Henderson (Bishop of Bath and Wells), circa 1960

Sir, Apropos your funeral satnav tale (letter, Feb 5), in 1967 a sign outside an undertaker's in Edgbaston read 'Do not enter box unless your exit is clear'.

The Times, 7 February 2014

GOODBYES

See you later, alligator.
In a while, crocodile.
In an hour, sunflower.
Gotta go, buffalo.
Chow, chow, brown cow.
See you soon, baboon.

Better swish, jellyfish.
Chop, chop, lollipop.
Gotta run, skeleton.
Bye, bye, butterfly.
Better shake, rattlesnake.
Say goodbye, said the fly.

Knowledge is knowing that a tomato is a fruit; wisdom is not putting one in a fruit salad.

Miles Kington (1941-2008), journalist, double bass player, broadcaster and inventor of Franglais. Quoted in The Independent

US baseball players with names that you would probably struggle to invent:

Madison Bumgarner	Razor Shines
Shooty Babitt	Boof Bonser
Cannonball Titcomb	Coco Crisp
Tim Spooneybarger	Rusty Kuntz (pron. 'koontz')
Pussy Tebeau	Catfish Hunter
Goose Gossage	Buckle Dent
Pickles Dillhoeffer	

Parents should consider names for their children carefully: I was at school with Crispin Winter and Robin Graves. In my regiment, were Ivor Burger and Justin Love. Twin cousins of mine were Sam and Ella – fortunately, three generations back. Maggie, my wife, was at school with Cherry Stone and Lavender Bush. The Islip Bridge Club near Oxford in 2015 was run by Justin Stead

I don't want to live on in the hearts of my countrymen; I want to live on in my apartment.

Heywood 'Woody' Allen (Born Allan Stewart Konigsberg) (b 1935), American actor, film maker, playwright and comedian. Three wives and three 'relationships'.

How many newspapers do you you need to cover a woman ?
No Observers, one Mail and as many Times as it takes.

Charlie Dunn, artist and poet

Riding is like nuts and bolts. If the rider is nuts, the horse bolts.

Nicholas Evans (b 1950), from 'The Horse Whisperer'

A consequence of a classical education has been an ability to read gravestone inscriptions and an enjoyment of latin jokes. Here are a few of the jokes:

Carpe diem – Frying tonight

Post hoc ergo propter hoc – A little more Niersteiner wouldn't hurt

Ad hoc – Wine not included

Non angli sed angeli – Fishing prohibited

Post mortem – Postal strike

Campos mentis – Mint sauce

Rara avis – Car hire not available

Noli tangere – I don't want to dance with you

Inter alia – An Italian airline

Quidquid in utra parte – £2 each way

Caesar adsum iam forte – Caesar had some jam for tea

Sic friatur crustum dulce – That's the way the cookie crumbles

The style and grammar guide of the Daily Express, compiled by the editor, Arthur Christianson, ended with the words 'All clichés should be avoided like the plague.'

It will be hard to find a man of his caliber.

Phineas Barnum (1810-1891), American showman and founder of Barnum and Bailey Circus, on the death of Zazel the Human Cannonball

How do you make anti freeze?
You take her blankets off.

Anon

UNDERWRITERS HAVE MESSAGE FROM NEW YORK THAT
VIRGINIAN IS STANDING BY TITANIC AND THAT THERE IS NO
DANGER OF LOSS OF LIFE. ISMAY

Telegram of April 14th 1912

*In January 1936, a young girl named Phyllis wrote to **Albert Einstein** to ask "Do scientists pray, and what do they pray for?"*

Dear Phyllis

I will attempt to reply to your question as simply as I can. Here is my answer:

Scientists believe that every occurrence, including the affairs of human being, is due to the laws of nature. Therefore a scientist cannot be inclined to believe that the course of events can be influenced by prayer, that is, by supernaturally manifested wish.

However, we must concede that our actual knowledge of these forces is imperfect, so that in the end the belief in the existence of a final, ultimate spirit rests on a kind of faith ... everyone who is seriously involved in the pursuit of science becomes convinced that some spirit is manifest in the laws of the universe, one that is vastly superior to that of man.

With cordial greetings,

Yours

Albert Einstein

Albert Einstein (1874-1955), German theoretical physicist. Developed general theory of relativity. Nobel Prize winner, organist and violinist

A woman is like a teabag. Only in hot water do you realise how strong she is.

*Nancy Reagan (1921-2016), actress, fashionable
First Lady of United States, 1981-1989*

~ 170 ~

Wild old men who give you jewels and sables,
Only live in Aesop's fables.
And when the tumult dwindled to a calm,
I left him practising the hundredth psalm.

George Gordon Byron (6th Baron Byron) (1788-1824), poet.
From The Vision of Judgement 1822

Always yield to temptation, it may not pass your way again

Clementina Graham (1782-1877), Scottish author and society hostess

Collective nouns seem to have come about in the Middle Ages for a number
of professions and people. These include:

A Rascal of Boys   A Sentence of Judges
A Gaggle of Gossips   An Eloquence of Lawyers
A Herd of Harlots   A Misbelief of Painters
A Skulk of Thieves   A Superfluity of Nuns
A Tabernacle of Bakers   A Discretion of Priests
A Drift of Fishermen

There are very many more that concern birds and animals and some of those
that amuse me are in the Countryside and Nature chapter.

Barbed wire was critical in controlling cattle in the American west and the
principle salesman and manufacturer was *John Warne Gates (1855-1911)*
industralist, gambler and president of The Texas Company (later Texaco).
His barbed wire slogan was "Lighter than air, stronger than whiskey,
cheaper than dust".

When you are courting a pretty girl, an hour seems like a second. But if
you sit on a hot stove for a second it seems like an hour. That is relativity.

Albert Einstein (1879-1955) German jewish theoretical physicist. Nobel
Prize in Physics. Acquired Swiss and American citizenship. Violinist

9 | Wordplay

Of all the world's languages, English is one of the richest for its vocabulary and its ability to give rise to many fascinating opportunities for the novel use of words. These are a few that have come my way and I have tried to classify them.

WORD SQUARES

Three-word squares are quite easy, such as:

```
S P Y
P I E
Y E T
```

But seven and over are very difficult to construct:

```
N E S T L E S
E N T R A N T
S T R A N G E
T R A I T O R
L A N T E R N
E N G O R G E
S T E R N E R
```

ANAGRAMS

Many collect anagrams and the best reflect in some way the word or words being anagrammed:

absence makes the heart grow fonder	–	he wants back dearest gone forever
the aristocracy	–	a rich Tory caste
astronomers	–	moon starers
circumstantial evidence	–	can ruin a selected victim
desperation	–	a rope ends it
HMS Pinafore	–	name for ship
one + twelve	–	two + eleven
Presbyterian	–	best in prayer
William Shakespeare	–	we all make his praise

ANTIGRAMS

astronomers	–	no more stars
funeral	–	real fun
festival	–	evil fast
marriage	–	a grim era

CRYPTOGRAMS

R O T A S
O P E R A
T E N E T
A R E P O
S A T O R

All the letters in Paternoster.

PALINDROMES

Rotas opera tenet Arepo sator
[Arepo the sower, guides that wheel with care]

Early Christian Palindrome

In girum imus noctes, et consumimur igni.
[We go wandering at night and are consumed by fire]

Νιψον ανομηματα μη μοναν υψιν
[Wash not only my face, but my transgression]

Around the dome of St Sophia, Istanbul.

As palindromes get longer they tend to lose sense but these four are sensible:

Sex at noon taxes.

Norma is as selfless as I am, Ron.

A man, a plan, a canal, Panama.

Doc note. I dissent, a fast never prevents a fatness. I diet on cod.

Peter Hilton (1923-2010) Professor of topological, homological and categorical algebra. Recruited aged 18 to Bletchley Park as a code breaker. Mason Professor of Pure Mathematics, Birmingham; Professor of Mathematics, Cornell; Professor of Mathematics, Washington; Louis Beaumont Professor at Cape Western; Emeritus Professor at Binghampton.

HOLORYMES

Lines of same sound, but different meaning:

> *Etonnamment monotone et lasse*
> *Est ton âme en mon automne, hélas!*

> *O! fragiles Hébreux! Allez, Rébecca, tombe!*
> *Offre à Gilles zèbres, oeufs; à l'Erèbe, hécatombe.*

*Both, **Victor Hugo** (1802-1885), French Romantic poet, novelist, dramatist. Elevated to peerage by King Louis-Philippe. Elected to National Assembly. Lived in exile in Guernsey following Napoleon III's coup d'etat. Made 4000 drawings. Buried in Pantheon*

THE ALPHABET

Alaric Watts (1797-1864) wrote a famous alphabetic poem in 1817 called 'The Siege of Belgrade'. Hard enough to alliterate, let alone rhyme.

An Austrian army awfully array'd,
Boldly by battery besieg'd Belgrade;
Cossack commanders cannonading come,
Dealing destruction's devastating doom.
Every endeavour engineers essay –
For fame, for fortune fighting – furious fray!
Generals 'gainst generals grapple – gracious God!
How honours Heav'n heroic hardihood –
Infuriate – indiscriminate in ill,
Kinsmen kill kindred, kindred kinsmen kill.
Labour low levels longest, loftiest lines –
Men march 'mid mounds, 'mid moles, 'mid murd'rous mines.
Now noisy noxious numbers notice naught,
Of outward obstacles opposing ought;
Poor patriots! partly purchas'd, partly press'd,
Quite quaking quickly, 'quarter, quarter,' quest.
Reason returns, religious right redounds,
Sorrow stops such sanguinary sounds.
Truce to thee, Turkey, triumph to thy train,

Unjust, unwise, unmerciful Ukraine,
Vanish vain vict'ry, vanish vict'ry vain. –
Why wish we warfare? Wherefore welcome were
Xerxes, Ximenes, Xanthus, Xaviere?
Yield, yield, ye youths, ye yeomen yield your yell;
Zeno's, Zorpater's, Zoroaster's, zeal
Attracting all, arms against acts appeal.

*And there is a well known Cockney alphabet, which spawned several
alternatives:*

A	for 'orses	Hay for horses
	for ism	Aphorism
	for gardener	Ava Gardner
B	for mutton	Beef or mutton
C	for highlanders	Seaforth Highlanders
	for yourself	See for yourself
	for miles	See for miles
D	for dumb	Deaf or dumb
E	for brick	Heave a brick
	for Bartok	Eva Bartok
F	for vescence	Effervescence
	for been had	Ever been had?
G	for police	Chief of police
H	for retirement	Itch for retirement
I	for Novello	Ivor Novello
	for lutin'	Highfalutin
	for an eye	Eye for an eye
J	for oranges	Jaffa oranges
K	for teria	Cafeteria
L	for leather	Hell for leather
M	for sis	Emphasis
N	for lope	Envelope
O	for the garden wall	Over the garden wall
	for a drink	Oh for a drink!
	for the wings of a dove	Oh for the wings of a dove

```
P   for a penny...................... Pee for a penny
Q   for buses ......................... Queue for buses
    for a song........................ Cue for a song
R   for mo............................. Half a mo'
    for sixpence ..................... Half a sixpence
    for Askey......................... Arthur Askey
S   for Williams .................... Esther Williams
T   for two............................ Tea for two
U   for 'mism ........................ Euphemism
V   for La France................... Vive la France!
    for la différence............... Vive la différence
W   for quits .......................... Double you for quits
X   for breakfast.................... Eggs for breakfast
Y   for husband..................... Wife or husband
    for biscuit........................ Wafer buscuit
Z   for breezes ...................... Zephyr breezes
```

TWISTERS

O to scuttle from the battle and to settle on an atoll far from
    brutal mortal 'neath a wattle portal!
To keep little mottled cattle and to whittle down one's
    chattels and not hurtle after brittle yellow metal!
To listen, non-committal, to the anecdotal local tittle-tattle
    on a settle round the kettle,
Never startled by a rattle more than betel-nuts a-prattle or
    the myrtle-petal's subtle throttled chortle!
But I'll bet that what'll happen if you footle round an atoll
    is you'll get in rotten fettle living totally on turtle, nettles,
    cuttle-fish or beetles, victuals fatal to the natal *élan-vital*,
And hit the bottle.
I guess I'd settle
For somewhere ethical and practical like Bootle.

Justin Richardson, The Sheldon Book of Verse, Book 3

I know our mythic history, King Arthur's and Sir Caradoc's,
I answer hard acrostics, I've a pretty taste for paradox.
I quote in elegiacs all the crimes of Heliogabalus,
In conics I can floor peculiarities parabolous.

Pirates of Penzance

To sit in solemn silence in a dull, dark dock,
In a pestilential prison, with a life-long lock,
Awaiting the sensation of a short, sharp shock,
From a cheap and chippy chopper on a big black block!

The Mikado

Here is Shakespeare:

Whereat, with blade, the bloody blameful blade,
He bravely broached his boiling, bloody breast.

A Midsummer Night's Dream

Children love these too:

A tutor who tooted the flute
Tried to tutor two tooters to toot.
Said the two to the tutor:
Is it harder to toot, or
To tutor two tooters to toot?

A flea and a fly in a flue
Were imprisoned, so what could they do?
Said the fly, 'Let us flee,'
Said the flea, 'Let us fly,'
So they flew through a flaw in the flue.

> *O Tite tute Tati tibi tanta tyranne tulisti!*
> [O tyrant Titus Tatius, what a terrible tumble you took]
>
> **Romulus** *on the assassination of Titus Tatius*

> *At tuba terribili sonitu tarantara dixit.*
> [But the trumpet in terrible tones trilled tarantara.]
>
> *Both quoted by Philip Howard in The Times*

And the French also:

> *Ton thé t'a-t'il ôté ta toux ?*
> [Has your tea relieved your cough?]

And one-liners:

> Mixed biscuits.
> Lemon liniment.
> Pre-shrunk silk shirt sale.
> Three short sword sheaths.
> The sixth sheikh's sixth sheep's sick.

PUNS

Thomas Hood's poem 'Faithless Nelly Gray' has a pun or two in each verse. These are four verses of many, the last two lines of the last verse being the ones we all remember.

> Ben Battle was a soldier bold,
> And used to war's alarms:
> But a cannon-ball took off his legs,
> So he laid down his arms!

> Now as they bore him off the field,
> Said he, 'Let others shoot,
> For here I leave my second leg,
> And the Forty-second Foot!'

So each one upwards in the air
His shot did he expend.
And may all other duels have
That upshot at the end.

His death, which happened in his berth,
At forty-odd befell:
They went and told the sexton, and
The sexton toll'd the bell.

Thomas Hood (1799-1845), poet, author and humorist

KNOCK, KNOCK

In the '70s there were a thousand 'Knock, Knock' jokes. Here are just two:

Knock, knock.
Who's there?
A little old lady.
A little old lady who?
I didn't know you could yodel.

Knock, knock.
Who's there?
Ammonia.
Ammonia who?
Ammonia a little boy who can't reach the doorbell.

SPOONERISMS

The Rev William Spooner (1844-1930), was Warden of New College, Oxford and notoriously prone to switching consonants or vowels. Most spoonerisms have never been authenticated.

I have always wanted to go to Poke Stoges.

Lady in a bus passing the village where Gray's Elegy was written

Lawfully loined together.

The (nameless) priest at a friend's wedding

Have another piece of
Grace, your Cake.

*Said to Cosmo Lang, Archbishop
of Canterbury by a nervous curate*

Here to speak on behalf of the Labour Party is Sir Stifford Crapps.

*A well known boob of **Macdonald Hobley**, the BBC announcer,
introducing a Party Political Broadcast in 1949*

Sir, In his letter to The Times (August 28) Sir Robin MacLellan suggests
that the occupant of a house named Dunchippin might be a retired
stonemason, fish frier, or an electronic wizard. Surely it is more likely that
he is an old golfer.

House names can often be misunderstood, as I discovered when I
noticed that a new friend's home was called Llamedos. I consulted my
Times Atlas only to find that no such place appeared to exist.

The mystery was solved when I realized that Llamedos spelt backwards
reflects a refreshing attitude to life in general and authority.

The Times, 2 September 1985

GARLANDS FROM LITERATURE

Lupin Pooter and Daisy Mutlar (Grossmiths); Hyacinth Robinson, Pansy
Osmond and Flora (James); Fleur Forsyte (Galsworthy); Buttercup
(Gilbert); Lobelia Sackville-Baggins (Tolkien); Aunt Dahlia (Wodehouse)
and Dahlia Fleming (Meredith); Amaryllis (Spenser); Madame Eglentyne
(Chaucer); Viola (Shakespeare); Rosa Klebb (Fleming); Rosa Dartle, Rosa

Bud and Flora Finching (Dickens); Poppy Carlyle (Mackenzie); Clover Carr (Coolidge); Rose of Sharon (Steinbeck); Magnolia Ravenal (Ferber); Uncle Pentstemon (Wells); Lavender Davis (Mitford) and Lavender Rolt (Pinero); Fuchsia Leach (Ouida); Flora Poste (Gibbons); Poppy Sellars (Priestley); Myrtle Wilson (Scott Fitzgerald); Ivy Eckdorf (Trevor); Tigerlily (The Rupert Annual); Marigold Spencer and Cherry Thomson (Lehmann); Cherry Boniface (Farquhar); and Zinnia, Petunia and Primrose Larkin (Bates).

Sir, Perhaps 'Dear Soeurs' might appeal to Mrs Walker (May 18) as an appropriate form of address, both on female and onomatopoeic grounds?

The Times, 1986. Following correspondence on
how to address two women living together.

I passed by Petra in a wink
It looked like Eaton Square – but pink.

Geoffrey Johnson

Finnegan's Wake is one long spelling mistake.
With not a lot
Of plot

*Attributed to **Ezra Pound** (1885-1972), expatriate American*
poet. Founder of Imagism.

The wind's in the willow,
Spring, dreaming for more;
The rat's on the river,
The toad's in the hole.

Ibid.

PUNCTUATION

A woman without her man is nothing

A woman: without her, man is nothing

Lynn Truss (b1955), writer and journalist

On the seeming absurdity of English language pronunciation:

Manet made so little monet,
Dealers thought it rather fonet
As for Monet, some (not Manet)
Thought he wasn't making anet.

*DB Wyndham Lewis (1882-1957), English co-founder of
Vorticist painting movement*

Two readers' contributions to a Spectator competition, December 1988

The Town of Milngavie
Can gladden the avie
And folk at Buccleuch
Will queuch for the veuch –
But the castle at Glamis
Has superior chamis.

So walk with me through
The broad avenough
With leaves 'neath our shoes
As we relish the voes
So loved by Defoe
There is so much to shoe
To one of esprit
So do come with mit.

John FN Wedge

If I could but choose,
I'd opt for a croose
On the waters of Oose
And dispel all my bloose.

After taking a snoose
The banks I'd peroose
And savour the vioose:
The rams and the eoose,
The young man who woose,
The lovers in toose . . .

How splendid to loose
All the bustle and quoose!
It's hard to walk
Through the streets of old Yalk!

Margaret Dews

Sir, The curator of the Tenby Museum has prepared a phonetic text of the Welsh national anthem to encourage singers on the terraces at rugby matches (letter, January 3).

But this text already exists, as those of us brought up in Wales, but too blinkered to learn Welsh, can testify.

The first line goes: 'My hen laid a haddock on Aunt Willie's knee.'

The Times, 6 February 1992

The German for 'one who assassinates the aunt of an African chieftain' is *ein Hottentottenpotentatentantentotenattentäter.*

The Times

Sir, Fortunately, the godmother of the Hottentot potentate did not die (Letters, February 7), although the attempt on her life – *Attentat* – is surely apocryphal.

Many years ago, however, I witnessed consternation when a client requested a *Kapitalertragssteuerfreistellungsbescheinigung* – a certificate of exemption from capital gains tax.

The task required completion of a *Kapitalertragssteuerfreistellungsbescheinigungantragsformular.*

Happily we found a supply of these in the *Kapitalertragssteuerfreistellungsbescheinigungantragsformularbehälter.*

The Times

The English try this too:

Pneumonoultramicroscopicsilicovolcanoconiosis – *the inhalation of very fine particles*

Antidisestablishmentarianism – *opposition to a link between Church and State.*

Floccinaucinihilipilification – *to estimate something as worthless*

Antitransubstantiationalist – *one who does not believe in transubstantiation*

FRENCH DEFINITIONS

Coup de grâce .... a lawnmower
Apéritif .... set of dentures
Pas de deux .... father of twins
Mal de mer .... sick of mother
Pièce de résistance .... fighting off an unwelcome advance
Esprit de corps .... embalming fluid
Ménage à trois .... small zoo
Métronome .... a little man living in the Underground

ROMAN EMPEROR'S NEMONIC

A truant calf calls noisily;
Great obstinate! Vile veal!
Thus dominating nervousness
Through hoarding apple-peel.
Mid-August come, persistently,
Don-Juans, sex-suffused,
Coerce mature hetairas
Anti-socially misused.

Go, go, my boys! Go pandering!
Descend green Arno's valley!
Give chase! Among those flowery peaks
Can't countless numbers dally?

The initial letters give the key to the Emperors:

Augustus, Tiberius, Caligula, Claudius, Nero,
Galba, Otho, Vitellius, Vespasian,
Titus, Domitian, Nerva,
Trajan, Hadrian, Antoninus Pius,
Marcus Aurelius, Commodus, Pertinax,
Didius Julianus, Septimius Severus,
Caracalla, Macrinus, Heliogabalus,
Alexander Severus, Maximin,
Gordian, Gordian, Maximus, Balbinus, Gordian, Philip,
Decius, Gallus, Aemilianus, Valerian,
Gallienus, Claudius, Aurelian, Tacitus, Florianus, Probus,
Carus, Carinus, Numerian, Diocletian.

This is the story of four people named Everybody, Somebody, Nobody and Anybody

There was an important job to be done and Everybody was sure Somebody would do it. Anybody could have done it but Nobody did it. Somebody got angry about that because it was Everybody's job. Everybody thought that Anybody could do it, but Nobody realised that Everybody would not do it. It ended up that Everybody blamed Somebody when actually Nobody accused Anybody.

ENGLISH WEATHER MONTHS

Snowy	Showery	Hoppy	Breezy
Flowy	Flowery	Croppy	Sneezy
Blowy	Bowery	Droppy	Freezy

Richard Brinsley Sheridan (1751-1816), Irish playwright. Owner of Theatre Royal. MP. Treasurer of the Navy

Correspondence in The Times in January 1995 produced these acronyms on the theme of Climbing Life's Ladder:

DINKYS	Dual income, no kids yet.
ORCHIDS	One recent child, heavily in debt.
TRIUMPH	Two rowdy infants, unemployed, middle-aged, planning hopefully
TRIFFIDS	Three recent infants, falling further into debt.
POFACED	Parents of four active children, endless debts.
POTS	Parents of teenagers.
KITBAGS	Kids in teens, bankrupt and grey.
FLOPSIES	Family left, on pension, suddenly Eldorado.
PLANTS	Pensioners looking after numerous toddlers.
TULIPS	Two used left over insolvent parents.
FAG ENDS	First adorable grandchildren, endlessly needing dosh.
TRIKING	Two retirement incomes, kids independent, no grandchildren.
TEPID	Tastes expensive, pension inadequate. Dammit
BIROS	Bedridden, income running out.
TOADS	Three offspring, all dependent still.
GUSSETS	Gave up sex, slowly edging towards solvency.
PIPS	Pensioners in penury.
COCOON	Cheap old childminder operating on nothing.

WORD BREAKS

...mans-
laughter

... to-
wed

... gene-
ration

... not-
iced

... ex-
porter

... one of the male-
factors

... the-
rapist

... the leg-
end of King Arthur's table

... no-
table

CROSSWORD CLUES

I used to collect crossword clues that I thought ingenious or amusing. They have been lost but three I recall are:

Naughty poet or the other way round (4,5) .... vice versa

Capital A followed by s (6) .... Athens

Sexual deviation of the deaf (5,2,4,4) .... prick up your ears

As if crossword setting was not difficult enough, some setters like to demonstrate their skills. This is such an example, from January 2014:

Across

7 — Bennett, playwright (4)
8 Infectious organisms (8)
9 Continent (6)
10 Ancient Greek city (6)
11 Distinctive atmosphere (4)
12 Spanish queen who was patroness to Columbus (8)
15 So to speak (2,2,4)
17 American wild cat (4)
18 Brian —, English science fiction writer (6)
21 —, Christie, novelist (6)
22 Italian composer; *non-alibi* (anagram) (8)
23 Mother (4)

Down

1 (On) hands and knees (3-5)
2 Heart condition (6)
3 Harsh in manner (8)
4 Deeds (4)
5 Ventilate (6)
6 Is not; am not; are not (4)
13 Prayer to the Virgin (3,5)
14 Form of cancer (8)
16 Unimportant details (6)
17 Colourless fluid in blood; green variety of quartz (6)
19 Sing using syllables (2-2)
20 (Greek) portico (4)

10 | Food and Drink

Madame Bollinger introducing the 1955 vintage:

Je le bois quand je suis heureuse et quand je suis triste. Quelquefois, je le bois quand je suis seule. Quand j'ai des invités, je le considère comme obligatoire. S'il fait chaud, il est rafraîchissant, et s'il fait froid, il me ragaillardit. Quand je n'ai pas faim, je le traite à la légère mais quand j'ai faim je le bois. Le matin, il est rafraîchissant et le soir il me relève. Autrement je ne le prends jamais, à moins d'en avoir soif.

[I drink it when I am happy and when I am sad. Sometimes, I drink it when I am alone. When I have guests, I consider it obligatory. If the weather is warm, it is cooling and if the weather is cold, it perks me up. I trifle with it if I am not hungry and drink it when I am. It is refreshing in the morning and picks me up in the evening. Otherwise, I never touch it – unless of course, I am thirsty.]

Madame Lilly Bollinger (1899-1977), French entrepreneurial classic Champagne maker

In victory I deserve Champagne; in defeat I need it.

Napoleon Bonaparte (1769-1821), Corsican born Emperor of France, political and military leader

Champagne is the only drink that improves a woman.

*Marquise Jeanne Antoinette Poisson (**Madame de Pompadour**) (1721-1764),*
Mistress of Louis XV, patron of the arts and champion of French pride

Three of the things I shall never attain
Envy, contentment and sufficient Champagne

Dorothy Parker *(1893-1967)(born Dorothy Rothschild). American writer,*
poet and satirist

Smirnoff vodka ran a series of ads in the '90s that suggested a fantasy if you
discovered Smirnoff – this spun many amateur variations:

Snow White thought 7-Up was a soft drink until she discovered
Smirnoff

I thought Wanking was a town in China until I discovered Smirnoff

I thought Plato was a Greek washing-up liquid until I discovered
Smirnoff

I used to think Fellatio was a character in Hamlet until I discovered
Smirnoff

I thought cirrhosis was a cloud until I discovered Smirnoff

A dessert without cheese is like a beautiful woman with only
one eye.

Jean-Anthelme Brillat-Savarin (1755-1896), French gastronome

Milk is rendered immortal in cheese.

Enoch Powell *(1912-1998), politician, MP, Minister of Health,*
Classical scholar, linguist and poet

Wine without cheese is like a kiss without a squeeze.

The noblest of all dogs is the hot-dog; it feeds the hand that bites it.

If the soup had been as warm as the wine, and the wine as old as the fish, and the fish as young as the maid, and the maid as willing as the hostess, it would have been a very good meal.

Attributed to **Duncan Hines** *(1880-1959), food critic.*
Quoted by Mark Forsyth in 'Elements of Eloquence', 2013

Writing in my sixty-fourth year, I can truthfully say that since I reached the age of discretion I have consistently drunk more than most people would say was good for me. Nor do I regret it. Wine has been to me a firm friend and a wise counsellor... Wine has made me bold but not foolish; has induced me to say silly things but not to do them.

Lady Diana Manners, Vicountess Norwich *(1892-1986) society hostess,*
author and intellectual

WINE

And what stuff, my dear boy. Everything that Hisse la Juppe had said proved true. What wines! Wines to set dimples in the cheeks of the soul. Some were little demure white wines, skirts lifted just above the knee, as it were. Others just showed an elbow or an ankle. Others were as the flash of a nymph's thigh in the bracken. Wines in sables, wines in mink! What an achievement for the French! Some of the range of reds struck out all the deep bass organ-notes of passions – in cultured souls like ours. It was ripping. We expanded. We beamed. Life seemed awfully jolly all of a sudden.

Lawrence Durrell *(1912-1990), novelist, poet, dramatic and travel writer.*
From 'Antrobus Complete', 1989

NUITS-ST-GEORGES 1964

Deep colour and big shaggy nose. Rather a jumbly, untidy sort of wine, with fruitiness shooting off one way, firmness another, and body pushing about underneath. It will be as comfortable and as comforting as the 1961 once it has pulled its ends in and settled down.

CHATEAU LYNCH-BAGES, GRAND CRÛ CLASSÉ PAULLIAC

Just the wine for those who like the smell of Verdi. Dark colour, swashbuckling bouquet and ripe flavour. Ready for drinking, but will hold well showing a gradual shift in style as it ages into graceful discretion.

*Extracts from 1968 wine catalogue of **Gerald Asher**, (b 1932) wine writer, wine merchant, Wine Editor of The Gourmet with entries published in five volumes. Based in California since 1974.*

Glaub, was wahr ist. Lieb, was rar ist. Trink, was klar ist.
[Believe what is true; love what is rare; drink what is clear]

On a 'Weinstübel' wall, Austria, 1958

Lord Mancroft (b 1957) Conservative peer and businessman remembers how Stephen Potter, (1990-1969), author, lecturer, elocution teacher 'Cockney accents cured' and inventor of One-Upmanship, once promoted a Cockburn 1897 which was clearly past its best. He spoke of:

The imperial decay of the invalid port... its gracious withdrawal from perfection... keeping a hint of former majesty, withal... whilst it hovered between oblivion and the divine *Untergang* of infinite recession.

A naïve little Burgundy without much breeding – I think that you will be amused by its presumption.

James Thurber (1844-1961), American humorist

Wine makes a man better pleased with himself.

Dr Samuel Johnson (1709-1784) essayist, poet and lexicographer

He could practise abstinence, but not temperance.

*Boswell on Johnson. **James Boswell**, 9th Lord of Auchinleck (1740-1795), Scottish biographer and lawyer. Samuel Johnson (known as Dr Johnson) (1709-1784) writer, poet, lexicographer, biographer. Compiler of* The Oxford Dictionary

Drink because you are happy, but never because you are miserable.

GK Chesterton *(1874-1936) writer, theologian, journalist*

A RECIPE FOR SALAD DRESSING

To make this condiment your poet begs
The pounded yellow of two hard-boil'd eggs:
Two boil'd potatoes, passed though kitchen sieve,
Smoothness and softness to the salad give.
Let onion atoms lurk within the bowl,
And, half-suspected, animate the whole.
Of mordant mustard add a single spoon,
Distrust the condiment that bites so soon:
But deem it not, thou man of herbs, a fault
To add a double quantity of salt:
Four times the spoon with oil of Lucca crown,
And twice with vinegar procur'd from town:
And lastly o'er the flavour'd compound toss
A magic soupçon of anchovy sauce.
Oh, green and glorious! Oh, herbaceous treat!
T'would tempt the dying anchorite to eat:
Back to the world he'd turn his fleeting soul,
And plunge his fingers in the salad bowl!

Rev Sydney Smith *(1771-1845), wit, writer and Anglican cleric. Sen Co Prae at Winchester College. Quoted in the Berry Bros wine catalogue of 1979*

When a new restaurant opened near Bromley in Kent, a critic wrote: 'Geographically, it is halfway between Elmer's End and Pratt's Bottom. Gastronomically, it is about the same'.

Widgeons, 2 Brinkley Street, London W1
This is another below par restaurant which seeks to impress with its over-long menu, napkins like blankets and Brobdingnagian wine glassses. The décor is red and overstuffed like the (mostly male) punters. The carpet pattern looks like a series of nose-bleeds. The food is a mess too. My pasta and woodland mushrooms had a whiff of marsh gas. My companion's lobster was a very nasty package with its overkill of coriander and vinaigrette and the cuttle fish risotto was as dry as the Kalahari. Sweetbreads with capers were OKish but unaccountably, they came with a tumulus of flaccid chips.

Restaurant review, 1922

In the kitchen the dirt was worse. It is not a figure of speech, it is a mere statement of fact to say that a French cook will spit in the soup – that is, if he is not going to drink it himself. He is an artist, but his art is not cleanliness. To a certain extent he is even dirty because he is an artist, for food, to look smart, needs dirty treatment. When a steak, for instance, is brought up for the head cook's inspection, he does not handle it with a fork. He picks it up in his fingers and slaps it down, runs his thumb round the dish and licks it

to taste the gravy, runs it round and licks again, then steps back and contemplates the piece of meat like an artist judging a picture, then presses it lovingly into place with his fat, pink fingers, every one of which he has licked a hundred times that morning. When he is satisfied, he takes a cloth and wipes his fingerprints from the dish, and hands it to the waiter. And the waiter, of course, dips his fingers into the gravy – his nasty, greasy fingers which he is for ever running through his brilliantined hair. Whenever one pays more than, say, ten francs for a dish of meat in Paris, one may be certain that it has been fingered in this manner. In very cheap restaurants it is different; there, the same trouble is not taken over the food, and it is just forked out of the pan and flung on to a plate, without handling. Roughly speaking, the more one pays for food, the more sweat and spittle one is obliged to eat with it.

George Orwell (Eric Blair) (1903-1950), novelist, committed to democratic socialism. From 'Down and Out in Paris', 1933

11 | Innuendo and Put Downs

There's nothing I like more on an evening like this than a long cool John Thomas. [*A cocktail of gin, lemon and sugar*]

Give a man a free hand and he'll run it all over you.

Mary 'Mae' West (1893-1980), American actress, singer, playwright and sex symbol

There, but for a typographical error, is the story of my life.

Dorothy Parker, *when told at a Hallowe'en party that people were ducking for apples*

Because he spills his seed on the ground.

When asked why she called her canary Onan

She was the original good time that was had by all.

Ruth 'Bette' Davis (1908-1989), *outstanding American actress. Of an available starlet*

THE HITE REPORT ON MALE SEXUALITY
September 1987 £12.50 (cased) / £9.95 (limp)

We are going to play a hiding and finding game. Now, are your balls high up or low down? Close your eyes a minute and dance around, and look for them. Are they high up? Or are they low down? If you have found your balls, toss them over your shoulder and play with them.

Nursery school games' mistress, 1976

Rugby is a game played by gentlemen with odd-shaped balls.

York University

New screwing method cuts fatigue and increases productivity.

Maintenance Engineering, 1997

Bright Young Thing: I liked your book. Who wrote it for you?
Woman writer: I'm glad you enjoyed it. Who read it to you?

Denise Robins: I've just written my 87th book.
Barbara Cartland: I've written 145.
Denise Robins: Oh, I see, one a year.

Denise Robins *(1897-1985) romantic novelist under pen names, published 170 novels (mostly with Mills & Boon) with sales of 100 million copies*

Barbara Cartland *(1901-2000), romantic novelist, published 723 novels (23 in one year) with sales of 750 million copies*

When asked in a BBC interview if she thought class barriers had broken down, Barbara Cartland replied: Of course they have or I wouldn't be talking to you.

I liked your opera. I think I will set it to music.

Beethoven *to fellow composer*

If he swallowed a nail, he would shit a corkscrew.

General Gerald Templer *(1898-1979), KG, GCB, GCMG, KBE, DSO Commander of Malaya Campaign, about Lord Louis Mountbatten (1900-1979) KG, GCB, OM, GCSI, GCIE, GCVO, DSO, PC, FRS, Supreme Commander, Southeast Asia*

12 | Billboards, Bumpers, Graffiti and Headlines

PEOPLE HAVE BEEN
sick CROSSING TO BOULOGNE
FOR 2,000 YEARS

Amended poster, Waterloo Station

WET PAINT
This is not an instruction

YOU CAN DO IT IN AN MG
Don't boast about your Triumphs

ROOM FOR ONLY SIX
PERSONS
or one opera
singer

*Amendment to notice in lift at
Sadler's Wells Theatre*

In the good old days, when
men were men and pansies
were flowers.

Darlington, NSW

Australia: where men are men and sheep are nervous.

Sex queen Fiona Richmond had promised to auction her knickers to raise cash for the children, but she had to let them down on the day.

The Mercury

Fiona Richmond (b 1945), glamour model, actress and sex symbol.
One time girlfriend of soft porn publisher Paul Raymond

A LITTLE COITUS NEVER HOITUS

New York City

WHERE WILL YOU BE ON THE DAY OF JUDGEMENT?
to which was added:
Still here, waiting for a No 95 bus

Church poster, South-East London

LECTURE THIS EVENING ON SCHIZOPHRENIA
to which has been added:
I've half a mind to go

and the further comment:
I'm in two minds also

Work for the Lord. The pay is terrible but
the fringe benefits are out of this world

Lavatory at Anglican theological college

MACARTHUR FLIES BACK TO FRONT

After a confrontation with President Truman in Washington

RECTITUDE IS A PAIN IN THE BUM

Edinburgh

ABSOLUTE ZERO IS COOL

Wimbledon

NUT SCREWS WASHERS & BOLTS

*Headline referring to a mental patient who raped two laundry workers
and escaped*

AVENUE ROAD
– what's wrong with the old one, then?

God is not dead, but alive and well and working on a much
less ambitious project.

IN THE BEGINNING
WAS THE WORD
AND THE WORD WAS
'AARDVARK'

EMMANUEL KANT
but Ghengis Khan

British Museum

Don't flatter yourself – stand nearer

Gents' lavatory, Sydney

80% OF BISHOPS TAKE THE TIMES
- the other 20% buy it

Inevitably, contraceptive machines invite graffiti:

My dad says they don't work.

Pull out knob to fullest extent and replace swiftly.

Port Isaac, Cornwall

This is the worst chewing gum I have ever tasted.

Not for sale during French postal strike.

Buy me and stop one.

If used on the premises, subject to VAT.

Go gay - it's cheaper.

IF OUT OF ORDER SEE THE LANDLORD.
And if it's in order, see the barmaid!

Should be used on every conceivable occasion

Spike Milligan

COLLETTE: GRAND OLD LADY OF FRENCH LETTERS

CHIP SHOP OWNER BATTERED MAN

Gateshead Post

BOOM AND BUST: DEMAND SAGS FOR BREAST IMPLANTS

The Times, February 2015

EIGHTH ARMY PUSH BOTTLES UP GERMANS

I once described a prominent Conservative – never mind which one – as having the vision of a mole, the passion of a speak-your-weight machine and the oratorical eloquence of a whoopee-cushion!

Bernard Levin (1928-2004), journalist, author, broadcaster and scholar. From 'Speaking Up', 1982

He is a self-made man and worships his creator.

John Bright (1811-1889), prominent Quaker and Member of Parliament

I've just learned about his illness. Let's hope it's nothing trivial.

Irvin S Cobb (1876-1944) American author and humourist

He is simply a shiver looking for a spine to run up.

Paul Keating (b 1944), Prime Minister of Australia

In order to avoid being called a flirt, she always yielded easily.

*Charles, Count Talleyrand (1754-1838), French bishop
and politician. Diplomatic aide to Napoleon*

He loves nature in spite of what it did to him.

Forrest Tucker (1919-1986), American film and television actor

He had delusions of adequacy.

Walter Kerr (1913-1966), American theatre critic

He has all the virtues I dislike and none of the vices I admire.

Winston Churchill (1874-1965)

I have never killed a man, but I have read many obituaries
with great pleasure.

Clarence Darrow (1857-1938), American Lawyer

Thank you for sending me a copy of your book. I'll waste no
time reading it.

Moses Hadas (1900-1966), American classical scholar

Sylvia Miles would go to the opening of an envelope.

Sylvia Miles (b 1932), American film and stage actress

I didn't attend the funeral, but I sent a nice letter saying I approved of it.

*Samuel Langhorne Clemens, known as **Mark Twain** (1835-1910), American author and humorist*

Her tossing muscles are prim and maintain their inhibitions, no matter how desperately they yearn for abandon.

__Cecilia Ager__ (1902-1986), American film critic and reporter for Variety on an unnamed opera star

If there was a fire in his library, it would destroy both his books, including the one he was still colouring.

__Richard Nixon__ (1913-1994), US President 1969-1974, on Dan Quayle (at the time a Senator, and later Vice President)

I am sitting in the smallest room of my house and have your book before me. It will shortly be behind me.

__Rev Sydney Smith__ (1771-1845) Cleric, critic and wit

Oscar Levant (actor-pianist): 'If you had it all over again, George, would you fall in love with yourself?'
George Gershwin: 'Oscar, why don't you play us a medley of your hit?'

__Oscar Levant__ (1906-1972), American composer, pianist (student of Schoenberg), actor and comedian

__George Gershwin__ (1889-1937), American/Lithuanian operatic, classical and popular pianist and composer

Waldo is one of those people who would be enormously improved by death.

__Saki__ (HH Munro) (1870-1916), humorous and reactionary writer. From 'The Feast of Nemesis', 1914

A smile is a curve that helps straighten things out.

Billboard, USA, 1963

Circumcision makes no difference to penile sensitivity, according to a story in The Jewish Chronicle. [*Thanks for the tip-off. Editor*]

MOVE. SHOOT. COMMUNICATE

On main gate of 3rd Field Battalion, Tanguyyi, Burma, 2017

13 | Legal

Judge: I'm tiring of your little jewels of Chancery learning.
Counsel: If your lordship will bear with me, I am about to cast
my last pearl.

Counsel: And is it true that your wife would sometimes beat
you with a clear impunity?
Witness: Er, no, it was mostly with a potato masher.

He that goes to law holds a wolf by the ears.

Robert Burton *(1577-1640), scholar, mathematician,*
astrologer and priest. From 'Anatomy of Melancholy', 1621

London stipendiary magistrate Eric Crowther writes in the current issue of the Magistrates' Association magazine of a woman convicted of soliciting who asked for time to pay her fine. 'How long do you need?' asked the bench. 'About 20 minutes should do', Crowther swears she replied.

The Times, 1986

Sir, Bernard Levin has chosen as his target that heavyweight of the media, the New York Times (for which read The Washington Post, or any other of the better-known US daily newspapers).

However, in looking forward to the first lawsuit arising from an accident in which the sheer weight of the newspaper resulted in injury, I regret to report that Mr Levin's research has let him down. It has already happened.

In a well-reported case, heard earlier this year, a woman successfully sued the Los Angeles Times for the loss of her dog. Apparently, a careless delivery boy hurled the offending newspaper into her garden, whereupon it landed on the unfortunate canine, leading to its instant demise. So much for the press hounds.

Letter to The Times, 1986

In an article regarding concerns about ageing judges, The Times legal correspondent Gary Slapper tells of a case in the Canadian courts.

> *Judge to defendant before sentencing:* "Have you anything to say?"
> *Defendant:* "Fuck all."
> *Judge to Clerk:* "What did he say?"
> *Clerk:* "He said 'Fuck all'."
> *Judge:* "Strange. I could have sworn I heard him say something."

Fiat iustitia, ruat caelum
[Let justice be done, even though the heavens fall in]

In a courtroom exchange, learned counsel FE Smith (later Lord Birkenhead), referred to the man in the dock as 'drunk as a judge'. He was interrupted by the judge who said, "I believe, Mr Smith, that the expression is 'drunk as a lord'", to which Smith rejoined: "As your lordship pleases."

There are three sides to each legal case: Yours, Theirs and the Truth.

The law that lawyers know about is Property and Land.
But why the leaves are on the trees,
And why the waves disturbes the seas,
Why honey is the food of bees,
Why horses have such tender knees,
Why winter comes when rivers freeze,
Why faith is more than what one sees
And hope survives the worst disease
And charity is more than these
They do not understand.

Hilary Pepler (1878-1951), printer, writer and poet. Quaker

Counsel: (seated and whispering) Please could you turn up the air conditioning. It's sweltering in here.
Usher: I'm sorry sir, I can't do that. It's controlled by the knob on the bench.

Professor Gary Slapper (1959-2016) Academic, educationalist, writer. The Times legal correspondent

Lawyers enjoy a little mystery. Why, if everybody came forward and told the truth, the whole truth and nothing but the truth, we should all retire to the workhouse.

Dorothy L Sayers (1893-1957) Scholar, crime writer, poet, playwright. First class degree in modern langauges at Oxford

14 | Advice

Advice is always dangerous, but good advice is fatal.

Oscar Wilde (1854-1898) Irish author, poet, playwright and wit

I always pass on good advice. It is the only thing to do with it.

Ibid. From An Ideal Husband, 1895

... the other reason why I have succeeded in life is that I never had any education. If you cram a boy's head full of other folk's ideas, where's the room for his own...

Graham Robertson (1894-1931), author, painter and collector. Portrait by Singer Sargent. From 'Time Was'

There are two things to aim at in this life; first to get what you want; and, after that to enjoy it. Only the wisest of men achieve the second.

Logan Pearsall Smith (1865-1946), American critic and essayist. From 'Afterthoughts', 1931

Thy friend has a friend and thy friend's friend has a friend. Be discreet.

The Talmud, book of Jewish law

Be civil to all; sociable to many; familiar with a few.

Benjamin Franklin (1706-1790), American 'Founding Father', polymath, author, scientist, statesman and diplomat. From 'Poor Richard's Almanac', 1759

Learning is often the enemy of initiative.

Lord Samuel (1870-1963), Liberal politician

I don't ask you to be unafraid; simply to act unafraid.

*Major **General Charles Gordon,** known as Gordon of Khartoum (1833-1885), military commander of Imperial Chinese Forces, Governor-General of the Sudan. Died in campaign against the Mahdi*

Regarding the F word – it is good as an exclamation but not as a comma.

Parent's advice to Ben Elton (b 1959), English-Australian comedian, author and actor

No one is at liberty to speak ill of another without a justifiable reason, even though he knows he is speaking the truth, and the public knows it too.

Cardinal John Newman (1801-1890), Anglican clergyman, Vicar of Oxford University Church. Later converted to Catholicism. From 'Apologia Pro Vita Sua'

Let not the Olive boast of her own fatness, nor the Fig-tree of her own sweetnesse, nor the Vine of her own fruitfulnesse, for we were all but Brambles.

John Donne (1572-1631), poet and Dean of St Paul's Cathedral

It's that middling sort, perched contentedly between brilliant success and outright failure, who are the most fortunate of mankind.

Robinson Crusoe to his son

Don't cry because it's over. Smile because it happened.

Theodor Seuss Geisel (1904-1991), American childrens' author and cartoonist better known as Dr Seuss

To laugh often and much; to win the respect of intelligent people and affection of children; to earn the appreciation of honest critics and endure the betrayal of false friends; to appreciate beauty; to find the best in others; to leave the world a little bit better, whether by a healthy child, a garden patch, or a redeemed social condition; to know even one life has breathed easier because you have lived. This is to have succeeded.

Ralph Waldo Emerson (1803-1882), American essayist and poet. Leader of the Transcendentalist movement

If you wish in the world to advance
Your merits you have to enhance
You must stir it and stamp it
And blow your own trumpet
Or trust me, you don't have a chance.

Sir WS Gilbert (1836-1911), dramatist, poet and producer of 14 comic operas with Sir Arthur Sullivan. From 'Iolanthe'

Whatever you can do or dream you can do, begin it. Boldness
has genius, power and magic. Begin it now.

Johann Wolfgang von Goethe (1749-1832), German poet and statesman

Read and forget
See and remember
Do and understand

Confucius (551–479BC), Chinese philosopher

It is better to light a candle than curse the darkness.

Chinese proverb

Muddy waters left to stand become clear.

Lao Tse (b. 904BC), Chinese Taoist philosopher

Hear twice before you speak once.

Scottish proverb

If you want to be happy for a few hours get drunk.

If you want to be happy for a few years get a wife.

If you want to be happy forever get a garden.

Beware that you do not lose the substance by grasping at the shadow.

Aesop (620-564 BC) Greek fabulist

Never marry for money. Divorce for money.

Wendy Liebman (b 1961) American comedienne and psychologist

Never wrestle with a strong man nor bring a rich man to court.

Roman proverb

15 | Politics, the Press and Journalism

Being President is like running a cemetery; you've got a lot of people under you but nobody is listening.

Bill Clinton (William Jefferson Blythe III) (b 1946), Rhodes Scholar, 42nd President of United States

There are only three men who have ever understood it (the Schleswig-Holstein question). One was Prince Albert, who is dead. The second was a German professor, who became mad. I am the third and I have forgotten all about it.

Viscount Palmerston (1784-1865), Member of Parliament, three times Foreign Secretary, Lord of the Admiralty, Lord of the Treasury

A politician: a man who would lay down your life for his country.

Those are my principles and if you don't like them I'll change them.

A politician

The Foreign Office: a hotbed of cold feet

An ambassador: an honest man sent abroad.

He is allowing his bleeding heart to rule his bloody nose.

Ernest Bevin (1881-1951), Trade Union leader and Labour Foreign Secretary. Said of an opposing minister in 1940

If you open that Pandora's Box, you never know what Trojan horses may get out.

Aneurin Bevan (1897-1960), Welsh politician. Minister for Health

I don't believe in black majority rule ever in Rhodesia... not in a thousand years.

Ian Smith (1919-2007), Prime Minister of Rhodesia, 1964. Rhodesia became independent in 1965 and changed its name to Zimbawe in 1979

Whenever a people, thirsting for liberty, discovers that its leaders will give it whatever it seeks, even to the point of intoxication, then if the Government resists its more extreme demands it is called tyranny, and those who show discipline to their superiors are called lackeys.

The father, filled with fear, comes to treat his son as equal and is no longer respected. The master no longer dares reprimand his servants and is mocked by them. The young claim the same consideration as the old, who in no way wishing to seem severe, yield to them.

In the name of liberty, no one is any longer respected. In the midst of this licence, there grows and flourishes a weed called tyranny.

Plato (428-348), Athenian philosopher and mathematician. From 8th book of 'The Republic'

We talked of different forms of government; and it was remarked what difficulties an excess of liberalism presents, as it calls forth the demands of individuals, and, from the quantity of wishes, raises uncertainty as to which should be satisfied. In the long run, over-great goodness, mildness, and moral delicacy, will not do, while underneath there is a mixed and sometimes vicious world to manage and hold in respect.

Johann Eckermann (1792-1854) German poet and author of 'Conversations with Goethe' 1998

Anyone who wants to get to the top has to have the guts to be hated. That applies to politicians, writers, anybody who gets into a certain position. Because that's how you get there. You don't get there by everybody loving you. Everybody in the world wants to be liked by everybody else. That's human nature. But you have to learn to take it.

Bette Davis (1908-1989) American film and stage actress. From 'The Lonely Life', 1962

People are always blaming their circumstances for what they are; I don't believe in circumstances. The people who get on in this world are the people who get up and look for the circumstances they want, and, if they can't find them, make them.

George Bernard Shaw (1856-1950), Irish playwright and critic. Founder of London School of Economics

What is the difference between the various political systems? H Williams' Chairman, John J Quin, gave his shareholders the following answer:

Socialism is when you have two cows and give one to your neighbour. Communism is when you have two cows and the state takes both and gives you milk. Fascism is when you have two cows and the state takes both and sells you milk. Nazism is when you have two cows and the state takes both and shoots you. Capitalism is when you have two cows, sell one and buy a bull. Bureaucracy is when you have two cows and the state takes both, shoots one, milks the other and pours the milk down the drain.

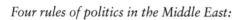

Four rules of politics in the Middle East:

1. Always keep the initiative
2. Always exploit the inevitable
3. Always keep in with the 'outs'
4. Never stand between a dog and a lamp-post

Stewart Perowne (1901-1989), British diplomat, historian and explorer. Married Freya Stark but a lover of young men in uniform

Democracy is the process by which people choose who to blame.

Bertrand Russell (1872-1970) Mathematician, historian, logician,
writer and political activist

The world is full of fools and fanatics who are always sure of themselves; wiser people are full of doubts.

ibid

It would be a very bad day for us when we admire our politicians. The Germans enormously admired Hitler. And look where it got them. The Italians thought Mussolini was wonderful. The Russians thought Stalin was wonderful. The great virtue of a democracy is that it always thinks its leaders are frightful. And it's an even greater virtue of a democracy that they always are.

AJP Taylor (1906-1990), historian and television presenter

A newspaper is of necessity something of a monopoly, and its first duty is to shun the temptations of a monopoly. Its primary office is the gathering of news. At the peril of its soul it must see that the supply is not tainted. Neither in what it gives nor in what it does not give, nor in the mode of its presentation, must the unclouded face of truth suffer wrong. Comment is free but facts are sacred.

CP Scott (1846-1932), publisher and journalist. First class degree in Greats
from Oxford. Editor and owner of Manchester Guardian

To the born editor, news is great fun, even as the capsizing of a boat in Sydney Harbour is great fun for the sharks.

George Bernard Shaw (1856-1950), Irish playwright and critic.

An editor is one who separates the wheat from the chaff, then prints the chaff.

Adlai Stevenson II (1900-1965)

Journalism consists largely in saying 'Lord Jones died' to people who never knew Lord Jones was alive.

GK Chesterton (1874-1936), theologian, poet, philosopher and critic

A modest little man with plenty to be modest about.

Claud Cockburn (1904-1986), Anglo-Scot journalist. About Prime Minister Attlee.

Believe nothing until it has been officially denied.

Ibid

The trouble about socialism is that eventually you run out of other people's money.

Margaret Thatcher (1925-2013), research chemist, barrister and Prime Minister

In politics, if you want anything said ask a man. If you want anything done, ask a woman.

Ibid

If my critics saw me walking over the Thames they would probably say it was because I couldn't swim.

Ibid

Making a speech on economics is like pissing down your leg. It may seem hot to you but never does to anyone else.

Lyndon B Johnson (1908-1973), 36th President of the United States, 1963-1969

He kept an open mind so long
That everything fell out
And false and true and right and wrong
Were scrambled into doubt.

Frances Hoare (née Hogg)

Truth wins when there is a free press.

Anon

We all know that prime ministers are wedded to the truth, but like some married couples they sometimes live apart.

HH Munro (known as Saki) (1870-1916) humorous novelist and story teller. From 'The Unbearable Bassington', 1912

A free society is where it is safe to be unpopular.

Adlai Stevenson (1835-1914), lawyer, US Vice President (1893-1897), Masonic Grandmaster. Married Letitia Green, founder of Daughters of the American Revolution

The corridors of power are always full.
Some get in by the door marked Push
And some get in by the door marked Pull.

CP Snow, Baron Snow (1905-1980), physical chemist and novelist. Scholarship to Christ College, Cambridge. Married to novelist Pamela Hansford Johnson

Power tends to corrupt and absolute power corrupts absolutely.

John Emerich Dalberg-Acton, 1st Baron Acton (1834-1902), politician and writer. Regius Professor of Modern History, Cambridge. Library of 60,000 books. Married Countess Ludmilla Euphrosina von Arco auf Valley

All power is agreeable and absolute power is absolutely agreeable.

Sir Osbert Lancaster (1908-1986), cartoonist, author, art critic and stage designer. 4th class degree but DLitt from Oxford

The Labour peer George Brown was well known for taking a tipple or two. An apocryphal (although unsubstantiated) story is that as foreign secretary on an official visit to Peru, he attended a musical soirée and stumbled up to an elegant figure glad in red and asked for a dance. "Mr Brown, I will not dance with you for three reasons," came the reply. "The first is that you are drunk, the second is that this is not a waltz but the Peruvian national anthem and thirdly, I am the Cardinal Archbishop of Santiago".

George Brown (Baron George-Brown) (1914-1985), Labour minister and Foreign Secretary

The trouble with fighting for human freedom is that one spends most of one's time defending scoundrels.

HL Menken (1880-1956), American journalist, satirist, critic and scholar. Anti-semite. Denounced the theory of relativity

Trying to maintain good relations with a communist is like wooing a crocodile. You don't know whether to tickle it under the chin or beat it over the head. When it opens its mouth, is it trying to smile or preparing to eat you?

Winston Churchill (1874-19 65), statesman, soldier, author, MP, Prime Minister (1940-1945, 1951-1955)

The extravagantly named Sir Hugh Vere Huntly Duff Munro-Lucas-Tooth was the First British MP to be born in the 20th Century and, at 21, was the youngest MP in Parliament.

It's not that we are against elections, we just like to know the results in advance.

Chinese official to **Chris Patten,** *Baron Patten of Barnes (b 1944) MP, last Governor of Hong Kong-'the whore of the east', Chairman of BBC Trust, Chancellor of Oxford University, first in modern languages at Oxford.*

We know what happens to people who stay in the middle of the road. They get run down.

Aneurin Bevan, *known as 'Nye' (1897-1960) Welsh miner, left wing politician, established National Health Service*

Conservatives often quote President Reagan's quip that the most terrifying words in the English language are "I'm from the government and I'm here to help".

In a Spitting Image sketch, Margaret Thatcher takes her cabinet out to dinner. "I shall have the steak" she says. "What about the vegetables?" asks the waiter. "They will have the same as me".

The requirements of the governor of the Bank of England are to have the tact of an ambassador and the guile of a Romanian horse thief.

Harold Lever, *Baron Lever of Manchester (1914-1995) Barrister and Labour politician*

In any moment of decision, the best thing you can do is the right thing. The next best thing is the wrong thing. The worst thing you can do is nothing.

Theodore Roosevelt *(1882-1945) 32nd President of the United States. Record of four presidential terms. Suffered from polio*

The Daily Mirror is read by those who think they run the country. *The Guardian* is read by those who think they *ought* to run the country. *The Times* is read by those who actually *do* run the country. *The Daily Mail* is run by the wives of those who run the country. *The Financial Times* is read by those who own the country. *The Morning Star* is read by those who think that the country should be run by another country. *The Daily Telegraph* is read by those who think it already is. And *The Sun* readers don't care who runs the country as long as she's got big tits.

Jim Hacker in 'Yes, Prime Minister'. Television satirical sitcom that ran for
38 episodes from 1980

Heckler: Speak up, I can't hear you.
Benjamin Disraeli: Truth travels slowly but it will reach even you in time.

Heckler: Don't you wish you were a man?
Agnes McPhail: Yes. Don't you?

Interviewer: "Do you have any skeletons in your cupboard?"
Alan Clark: "Dear boy, I can hardly close the door".

Alan Clark (1928-1999) Flamboyant right wing politician, diarist,
barrister, military historian

16 | Old age and Death

Malcolm Muggeridge on first becoming aware of the onset of old age:

'Being then, well past my allotted span of three score years and ten, as the old do, I often wake up in the night and feel myself in some curious way, half in and half out of my body, so that I seem to be hovering between the battered old carcass that I can see between the sheets and seeing in the darkness and in the distance a glow in the sky, the lights of Augustine's City of God. In that condition, when it seems just a toss-up whether I return into my body to live out another day, or make off, there are two particular conclusions, two extraordinarily sharp impressions that come to me. The first is of the incredible beauty of our earth – its colours and shapes, its smells and its features; of the enchantment of human love and companionship, and of the blessed fulfilment provided by human work and human procreation. And the second, a certainty surpassing all words and thoughts, that as an infinitesimal particle of God's creation, I am a participant in his purposes, which are loving and not malign, creative and not destructive, orderly and not chaotic, universal and not particular. And in that certainty, a great peace and a great joy.'

Richard Ingrams (b 1937), editor of Private Eye.
From 'Muggeridge – a biography', 1995

On 8th September 1882
He left us in peace

Gravestone in San Michele

OBITUARY NOTICES

Smith, Ronald Charles Albert died on 7th October 2014. 87 years, a pleasurable lifestyle and a questionable fitness level, have seemingly contributed to a loss of balance and I have fallen off the perch. A party is planned for relatives and friends (and enemies wishing to clear their conscience); announcement in due course, tickets free on application. Cremation has taken place, so no flowers, prayers, hymns or other 'old toffee', just a good party and plenty of laughter. I shall be sorry to miss it! Donations to the British Racing Drivers' Club Benevolent Fund, the Brain and Spine Foundation or the Mark Hanna Specialist Foundation.

The Times, 12 November 2014

Cohen, Dolly, much loved if often maddening mother of David, grandmother of Nicholas and Reuben, ex-mother-in-law of Aileen, mother-in-law of Julia, sister to Laura and Ella, aunt of Francine, friend of Evi, died on March 25th in London. She will be missed in all her many sided humanity. She will never surprise us again with a remarkably apposite quote from Molière or Heine or her knowledge of the law or nag us to get our hair cut or switch from English to German to Hungarian in the course of a sentence. May her soul rest in peace, with her parents, as she prayed for.

The Times, 28 March 1997

Lloyd, Nigel Peregrine, aged 79, found lasting peace on leaving his wife Janice, daughter Claudia and his sister Susan.

The Times, 11 December 2010

Barrington, Valerie Mary... she lived with her husband for 50 years and died in the confident hope of a better life.

The Times, 17 November 2016

Death is not extinguishing the light but blowing out the candle because the dawn has come.

Sir Rabindranath Tagore (1861-1941), Bengali polymath and Nobel Prize winner. Quoted in a letter following my mother's death. She had met Tagore in India

As you love me let there be no mourning when I go. Rather of your sweet courtesy rejoice with me at my soul's loosing from captivity.

Sir Walter Raleigh (1552-1618) writer, poet, politician, courtier, spy and explorer

Find time to smell the daisies before you push them up.

Lectore, si monumentum requiaris circumspice.
[If you seek a monument look around you.]

Epitaph in St Paul's Cathedral of Sir Christopher Wren (1632-1723), architect

O Lord support us all the day long of this troublous life, until the shadows lengthen and the evening comes, the busy world is hushed, the fever of life is over, and our work is done. Then, Lord, in Thy mercy, grant us safe lodging, a holy rest and peace at the last.

Book of Common Prayer

He burns his candle at both ends
It will not last the night.
But oh my enemies, oh my friends
It gives a lovely light.

Edna St. Vincent Millay (1892-1950), American playwright, Pulitzer Prizer winner for poetry, feminist and serial lover. From magazine 'Poetry', June 1918

She took her bright candle
And went into another room I cannot find.
But I knew she was here
Because of all the love she left behind.

Old Chinese verse

'What would you really die for?'
'Immortality.'

'Woody' Allen (b 1935), American actor, writer, film director,
comedian and playwright

GOD'S LENT CHILD

I'll lend you for a little while a child of mine, God said,
For you to love the while she lives, and mourn for when she's dead.
It may be six or seven years, or forty two or three,
But will you, 'till I call her back, take care of her for me?
She'll bring her charms to gladden you. And should her stay be brief,
You'll always have your memories as solace in your grief.
I cannot promise she will stay, since all from earth return,
But there are lessons taught below I want this child to learn.
I've looked this whole world over in my search for teachers true,
And from the folk that crowd life's lane, I have chosen you.
Now will you give her all your love and not think the labour vain,
Nor hate me when I come to take this lent child back again.
I fancy that I heard them say, 'Dear God Thy will be done',
For all the joys this child will bring, the risk of grief we'll run.
We will shelter her with tenderness, we'll love her while we may,
And for all the happiness we've ever known, we'll ever grateful stay.
But should the angels call her much sooner than we'd planned,
We will brace the bitter grief that comes and try to understand.

William Congreve *(1670-1729), lawyer, playwright*

If I lie down upon my bed I must be here,
But if I lie down in my grave I may be elsewhere.

Florence Smith, known as Stevie, (b 1902), novelist and poet

At death we may have the surprise of our lives.

John Stewart Collis (1900-1984)

Where 'er you walk, cool gales shall fan the glade;
Trees, where you sit, shall crowd into a shade.
Where 'er you tread, the blushing flowers shall rise.
And all things flourish where 'er you turn your eyes.

George Frederick Handel (1685-1759). From the opera Semele, 1743

ARTHUR GASCOYNE CECIL

British political life will be the poorer for the loss of Robert Arthur Gascoyne Cecil, fifth Marquess of Salisbury, who has died, aged 78. Since the Cecils made such a tremendous intellectual comeback at the turn of the century, they have produced scions with minds like razors, with exquisitely sensitive souls, and with rugged opinions, the whole encased in curiously frail-looking corporeal tenements.

Sir Colin Reith Coote (1893-1979), Daily Telegraph Editor, Liberal MP

Sign outside church of St Bartholomew:
JESUS DIED FOR YOUR SINS
Wife passing by with husband: 'Now look what you've done.'

There comes a time when you no longer hope to improve things, you just try to keep them going.

Auberon Waugh (1939-2001), author and journalist.
Rusticated from Oxford

If I should die and leave you here a while
Be not like others, sore, undone, who keep
Long vigils by the silent dust and weep.
For my sake, turn again to life and smile
Leaving thy heart and tender hand to do
Something to comfort other hearts than mine.
Complete those dear unfinished tasks of mine
And I, perchance, may therein comfort you.

Mary Lee Hall (1843-1927), American lawyer, suffragette and
philanthropist

There is not enough darkness in the world to quench the light
of this one small candle.

On a tablet in memory of Jimmy – a marmoset – beside the Henley
bypass. Quoted by Lucinda Lambton, Lady Worsthorne (b 1943), writer,
photographer and broadcaster, in a TV programme on animal memorials

An advantage of being older is that one hopes less and minds less.

Malcolm Muggeridge (1903-1990), journalist, author, satirist and spy

Life is so short and death so certain, and when death comes, the silence and
separation are so complete, that one can never make too much of the ties
and affections and relationships that bind us to the living.

Marie Belloc Lowndes (1868-1947). Wrote 'The Lodger', based on the
Jack the Ripper murders, which has been made into a film five times

RA – All the beautiful time is yours for always, for it is life that takes away,
changes and spoils so often – not death, which is really the warden and
not the thief of our treasures.

From the 'In Memoriam' columns of The Times

'There are many virtues in growing old.' He paused, he swallowed, he wet his lips, he looked about. The pause stretched out, he looked dumbstruck! The pause became too long, far too long. He looked down, studying the table top. A terrible tremor of nervousness went through the room. Was he ill? Would he ever be able to get on with it? Finally he looked up and said, 'I'm just trying to think what they are'!

Somerset Maugham (1874-1965), playwright, novelist, doctor and spy.
From 'Rain', 1921

Do not go gentle into that good night
Old age should burn and rave at close of day.
Rage, rage against the dying of the light.

Dylan Marlais Thomas (1914-1953), Welsh poet and author

ODE TO LIFE

Life! I know not what thou art,
But know that thou and I must part;
And when, or how, or where we met,
I own to me's a secret yet.
But this I know, when thou art fled,
Where 'er they lay these limbs, this head,
No clod so valueless shall be
As all that then remains of me.

Life! we've been long together,
Through pleasant and through cloudy weather;
'Tis hard to part when friends are dear;
Perhaps 'twill cost a sigh, a tear; –
Then steal away, give little warning,
Choose thine own time;
Say not 'Good-night', but in some brighter clime
Bid me 'Good-morning'!

Anna Laetitia Barbauld (1743-1825), English poet fluent in six languages.
Married the Huguenot, Rochemont Barbauld

I have outlived my youthfulness
So a quiet life for me.
Where once I used to scintillate,
I sin till ten past three.

Roger McGough (b 1937), poet, broadcaster and playwright

For when the One Great Scorer comes to write against your name,
He marks – not that you won or lost – but how you played the game.

Henry Grantland Rice (1880-1954), American sportswriter.
The last two lines of 'Alumnus Football', 1908

When as a child I laughed and wept,
    Time crept.
When as a youth I dreamed and talked,
    Time walked.
When I became a full grown man,
    Time ran.
And later as I older grew,
    Time flew.
Soon shall I find when travelling on,
    Time gone.
Will Christ have saved my soul by then?
    Amen.

Inscribed on the pendulum of the clock at St Lawrence's Church,
Bidborough, Kent

Every old man that dies is a library that burns.

AH Ba

If I must die, I will encounter darkness like a bride
And hug it in mine arms.

Scene I, Measure for Measure

Injurious time now with a robber's haste
Crams his rich thieving up, he knows not how:
As many farewells as there be stars in heaven,
With distinct breath, and consign'd kisses to them,
He fumbles up into a loose adieu,
And scants us with a single famished kiss,
Distasted with the salt of broken tears.

Scene IV, Troilus & Cressida

Bob Hope (1903-2003) British-American comedian, actor, singer, dancer, athlete and author, when asked what he wanted played at his funeral, replied: 'Surprise me!'

The smallest coffins are the heaviest.

Youth is a state of mind – not a time of life. It is the freshness
of the deep springs of Life.

Samuel Ullman (1840-1924), American poet and humanitarium

People do not grow old merely by the passing years; they age
when they desert their ideas.

Ibid

There are not stars but openings in Heaven where the love of
those lost pours through to confirm that they are happy.

Inuit saying

'How old would you say I was?'
'I've no idea.'
'Eighty-one.' He waited for some rebuttal.

Anita Brookner (b 1928), novelist and art historian

You are as young as your faith, as old as your doubt; as young as your self-confidence, as old as your despair; as long as your heart still receives messages of beauty, hope, cheer, courage and power from God and your fellow men – then you are young.

Douglas MacArthur (1880-1964), American general, Field Marshal of Philippine Army. Medal of Honor, DSC twice, Silver Star seven times. Supreme Commander of Pacific 1942

The worst thing about getting old is feeling young.

Oscar Wilde (1854-1900) playwright, novelist, poet and wit

Don't stop doing things when you're growing old, because you'll only grow old when you stop doing things.

Dame Thora Hird (1911-2003), actress, three BAFTAs, appeared in 100 films

I'M VERY WELL THANK YOU

There is nothing the matter with me,
I'm healthy as I can be,
I have arthritis in both my knees,
And when I talk – I talk with a wheeze.
My pulse is weak, and my blood is thin,
But – I'm awfully well for the shape I'm in.

Arch supports I have for my feet
Or I wouldn't be able to walk in the street;
Sleep is denied me night after night,
But every morning I find I'm alright.
My memory's failing, my head's in a spin.
But – I'm awfully well for the shape I'm in.
The moral is this – as my tale I unfold –
That for you and for me who are growing old,
It's better to say 'I'm fine' with a grin,
Than to let folks know the shape we are in.
How did I know that my youth is all spent?
Well, my 'get up and go' has got up and went!

But I really don't mind when I think with a grin
Of all the grand places my 'get up' has been.
Old age is golden I've heard it said,
But sometimes I wonder as I get into bed,
(With my ears in the drawer, my teeth in a cup,
My eyes on the table) – until I get up.

Ere sleep overtakes me I say to myself,
Is there anything else I could lay on the shelf?
When I was young my slippers were red,
I could kick my slippers right over my head;
When I was older my slippers were blue,
But still I could dance the whole night through.

Now I am old my slippers are black;
I walk to the shops and puff my way back;
I get up each morning and dust off wits
And pick up the paper to read the 'Obits';
If my name is not there I know I'm not dead;
So I have a good breakfast — and go back to bed!

Constance O'Neon, Scottish poet c. 1953

The kiss of the wind for lumbago
The stab of the thorn for mirth
One is nearer to death in a garden
Than anywhere else on earth

Voltaire on his deathbed was advised to renounce the devil. He replied: 'Now is not the time to make enemies.'

Francois-Marie Arouet, known as **Voltaire** (1694-1778), French author, philosopher, historian, poet and wit

On hearing the news that President Calvin Coolidge had died, Dorothy Parker exclaimed: 'How could they tell?'

COMMENDATION

Go forth upon your journey from this world, in the name of God the Father who created you; in the name of Jesus Christ who redeemed you; in the name of the Holy Spirit who sanctifies you.

May the angels of God greet you and the saints of God welcome you. May your rest be this day in peace and your dwelling in the paradise of God.

'The Proficiscere.' Used by Elgar in The Dream of Gerontious, 1900

As for me, my life is already being poured out on the altar and the hour for my departure is upon me. I have run the great race, I have finished the course, I have kept the faith. And now there awaits me the garland of righteousness which the Lord, the righteous judge, will award me on the great day, and not to me alone but to all who have set their hearts on his coming.

2 Timothy 4:6-8

The Glory of Life is to give and not to get, to serve not to be served, to love and not to be loved, to be a strong hand in the dark to another in the time of need, and to be a cup of strength to any soul in a crisis of weakness. This is to know the Glory of Life.

If I be the first of us to die
Let not grief blacken long your sky.
Be bold yet modest in your grieving.
There is a change but not a leaving.
For just as death is part of life,
The dead live forever in the living.

Nicholas Evans (b 1950), journalist, novelist (of The Horse Whisperer, 1995). First class Oxford law degree, screenwriter and film producer.

So when you walk the wood where once we walked together
And scan in vain the dappled bank beside you for my shadow,
Or pause where we always did upon the hill to gaze across the land
And spotting something, reach by habit for my hand,
And finding none, feel sorrow start to steal upon you,
Be still. Close your eyes. Breathe.
Listen for my footfall in your heart.
I am not gone but merely walk within you.

Ibid

When I am dead, shed no sad tears for me. First, give God thanks for all the joys of life and for all the gifts he heaped upon my soul. For so much love, both human and divine; for eyes that see the beauty in the world; for ears that hear the earth's song. Above all else for knowing that God is God; for wonder in the human life of Christ; for revelation of the truth of truth; the trinity of power, mercy, love. Give thanks that one as mean as I should know the generosity of God.

Found in my mother's desk after her death. Author unknown

Keep alive in our hearts, O Lord, the adventurous spirit which makes me scorn the way of safety; for only can we be followers of those gallant souls who in every age have ventured in obedience to the call and for whom the trumpets have sounded on the other side.

WHAT IS SUCCESS?

He has achieved success who has lived well, laughed often and loved much;
Who has enjoyed the trust of good women, the respect of intelligent men and the love of children;
Who has left the world a better place than he found it, whether by an improved poppy, a perfect poem or a rescued soul;
Who has always looked for the best in others and given the best he was able;
Who never lacked appreciation of earth's beauty or failed to express it;
Whose life was an inspiration;
Whose memory is a benediction.

Bessie A Stanley (1879-1952), the winner of a competition held by Brown Book Magazine in 1904 to answer the question What is Success? in less than 100 words

The dead don't die – they look on and help

DH Lawrence (1885-1930), novelist, playwright, literary critic and painter

HERACLITUS

They told me Heraclitus, they told me you were dead,
They brought me bitter news to hear and bitter tears to shed.
I wept, as I remembered how often you and I
Had tired the sun with talking and sent him down the sky.

And now that thou art lying, my dear old Carian guest,
A handful of grey ashes, long, long ago at rest,
Still are the pleasant voices, they nightingales awake;
For Death, he taketh all away, but them he cannot take.

Epitaph of Heraclitus (535-475), Greek philosopher, by Callimachus of Cyrene, 200BC. Translated by William Cory, (1823-1892), Eton schoolmaster

REFLECTION

I used to think, loving life so greatly, that to die would be like leaving a party before the end. Now I know that the party is really happening somewhere else; that light and the music, escaping in snatches to make the pulse beat and the tempo quicken, come from a long way away. And I know too that when I get there the music will never end.

Evangeline Paterson (1928-2000), poet

I thank thee God that I have lived in this great world and known its many joys. The song of birds, the strong sweet scent of hay on cooling breezes, the flaming sunsets at the close of day. Hills and the lonely heather covered moors, music at night and the moonlight on the sea. The beat of waves upon a rocky shore and wild, white spray flung high in ecstasy. The faithful eyes of dogs and treasured books, the love of kin and fellowship of friends and all that makes life beautiful.

... I know there is yet to come an even richer and more glorious life and most of all because your only Son once sacrificed life's loneliness for me. I thank you God that I have lived.

Elizabeth Craven (Margravine of Brandenburg-Ansbach) (1750-1828), author, traveller and socialite

You can shed a tear that she is gone,
or you can smile that she has lived.

Your heart can be empty that you cannot see her,
or it can be full of the love you shared.

You can remember her and only that she has gone,
or you can cherish her memory so that it lives on.

You can cry and close your mind,
or you can do what she would want: dry your eyes, smile, love and go on.

David Harkins (b 1958), painter and poet. Poem chosen to be read at the funeral of Queen Elizabeth the Queen Mother

In St Mary's church at Wraxall, Dorset is a monument to William Lawrence, 1681. It reads:

> Welcome dear death let sweetest sleep here take me
> In thy cool shades and never more awake mee
> Like a rich cortege draw thy darkness round
> Like a closed chamber make my grave profound
> In it I'le couch secure no dreams affright
> A silent lodger here no cares to bite
> Making thy bed seeme hard or long they night
> Let not the armes Oh grave yet still enfold mee
> Alas think not thou canst forever hold mee
> Weel'le breake at length thy marble wombe asunder
> Reissue thence and fill the world with wonder
> Envy thou'll then see the Power divine
> Nevre digge his diamonds from they deepest myne
> Cleanse cleare and polish them and then shall by farre
> Each dust of theirs outshine the morning starre

Here Lie The Souls Of Men Brushed By The Winds Of Eternity

Words on the war graves' memorial of the Battle of the Somme

Bring us O Lord, at our last awakening into the house and gate of heaven, to enter into that gate and dwell in that house, where there shall be no darkness nor dazzling but one equal light; no noise nor silence, but one equal music; no fears nor hopes but one equal possession; no ends nor beginnings but one equal eternity in the habitations of they glory and dominion.

John Donne (1573-1631)

> But at my back I always hear
> Time's winged charriot hurrying near.
> And yonder, all before us lie
> Deserts of vast eternity

*Andrew Marvell (1621-1678), metaphysical poet
(in Latin and Greek), satirist and politician*

17 | Epitaphs and Tributes

No man is an Iland, intire of it selfe; every man is a peece of the Continent, a part of the maine; if a Clod bee washed away by the Sea, Europe is the lesse, as well as if a Promontorie were, as well as if a Mannor of thy friends or of thine owne were; any mans death diminishes me, because I am involved in Mankinde; And therefore never send to know for whom the bell tolls; it tolls for thee.

John Donne (1572-1631), poet and cleric. From 'Devotions', 1624

John Donne, Anne Donne, undone.

John Donne married scandalously and for love against the wishes of Anne's father. This was socially disastrous. Donne spent time in prison, lost his job and sued his father-in-law to get the marriage declared valid. They had 12 children before Anne died aged 33.

To Hilaire Belloc
    Success, as very well you know,
    Is not becoming rich and swell,
    But doing what you meant to do,
    And doing it supremely well.

Duff Cooper (1890-1954), Viscount Norwich, husband of Lady Diana Cooper and father of John Julius Norwich

To Duff Cooper
    From quiet homes and first beginning,
    Out to the undiscovered ends,
    There's nothing worth the wear of winning,
    But laughter and the love of friends.

Hilaire Belloc (1870-1953), Anglo-French writer and historian

*In 1949 **Duff Cooper** brought out a privately printed volume of Translations and Verses, which bore testimony to his talents and contained the most beautiful of all his poems to Diana. It was a gift for her on their twenty-ninth wedding anniversary in 1948:*

> Fear not, sweet love, what time can do;
> Though silver streaks the gold
> Of your soft hair, believe that you
> Can change but not grow old.
> Though since we married, twenty-nine
> Bright years have flown away.
> Beauty and wisdom, like good wine,
> Grow richer every day.
> We will not weep, though spring be past,
> And autumn's shadows fall,
> These years shall be, although the last,
> The loveliest of all.

> This perishable stone marks the grave of
> DUFF COOPER
> whose name is imperishable in the memory of
> England and of those who loved him.
> Attached to this world but free of its trammels
> he loved the light and did not fear
> the coming of the dark.

*Epitaph written by **Diana Cooper***

Of Lady Diana Manners (youngest daughter of Duke of Rutland) aged 22. Later Viscountess Norwich, wife of Duff Cooper. Actress, socialite member of the intellectual group The Coterie:
She has a flashing mind and dazzling skin; her wit illuminates her complexion like forked lightning playing on a bowl of cream, and her beauty sweetens her wit like honey on the point of a dagger.

Anthony Asquith (1902-1968), Wykehamist and film maker

Quick, serve the dessert! I think I am dying!

> *Paulette Brillat-Savarin, (sister of the lawyer and gastronome*
> *Jean Anthelme Brillat-Savarin, 1755-1826). Said to have died*
> *on her 100th birthday*

Eat dessert first

> *Ernestine Ulmer (1893-1987), American author*

She's as tough as an ox. She'll be turned into Bovril when she dies.

> *Of a friend*

My exit is the result of too many entrées.

> *Richard Monckton-Milnes (1809-1885), 1st Baron Houghton, FRS.*
> *Poet and politician*

A man of much courage and superb equipment.

> *On Brigham Young (1801-1877), the Mormon leader, who died*
> *leaving seventeen or more wives*

This wallpaper is killing me. One of us must go.

Oscar Wilde (1854-1900)

Am I dying or is this my birthday?

Nancy Astor (1879-1964), American born socialite and Member of Parliament. When all her children assembled by her deathbed

Don't get rid of my devils for my angels may go too.

WH Auden *(1907-1973), Anglo-American poet*

Respect this place, this hallowed ground.
A legend here, his rest has found.
His feet would fly, our spirits soar.
He earned our love for evermore.

Inscription on the grave of Red Rum, (1965-1995) buried by the winning post of Aintree Racecourse. Unmatched steeplechaser who won the Grand National three times and twice came second

Maggie, my wife, has chosen this as her epitaph:

Here lies a poor woman who was always tired,
She lived in a house where help was not hired.
Her last words on earth were "Dear friends I am going
Where washing's not done nor sweeping nor sewing,
But everything there is exact to my wishes;
For where they don't eat, there's no washing of dishes,
I'll be where loud anthems will always be ringing,
But having no voice I'll be clear of the singing.
Don't mourn for me now, don't mourn for me never,
I'm going to do nothing for ever and ever".

Rose Henniker Heaton (d 1932). Australian author and wife of Sir John Henniker Heaton MP. From The Perfect Hostess, 1931

*On the day of her death in March 1941, **Virginia Woolf**'s husband Leonard discovered this letter on the mantlepiece. Virginia's body was found weeks later in the River Ouse, the pockets of her coat filled with stones. She had endured a lifetime of mental illness.*

Dearest

I feel certain that I am going mad again. I feel we can't go through another of those terrible times. And I shan't recover this time. I begin to hear voices, and I can't concentrate. So I am doing what seems the best thing to do. You have given me the greatest possible happiness You have been in every way all that anyone could be. I don't think two people could have been happier till this terrible disease came. I can't fight any longer. I know I am spoiling your life, that without me you could work. And you will I know. You see I can't even write this properly. I can't read. What I want to say is I owe all the happiness of my life to you. You have been entirely patient with me and incredibly good. I want to say that – everybody knows it. If anybody could have saved me it would have been you. Everything has gone from me but the certainty of your goodness. I can't go on spoiling your life any longer.

I don't think two people could have been happier than we have been.

V

Taken from Letters of Note, compiled by Shaun Usher, 2013

To live defeated and inglorious is to die daily.

Napoleon Bonaparte (1769-1821)

Patriotism is a lively sense of collective responsibility. Nationalism is a cock crowing on its own dunghill.

Richard Aldington (1892-1962), poet, novelist and biographer. Member of the Imagist and Futurist movements

Life is a moderately good play with a badly written third act.

Truman Capote (1924-1984), American novelist, screenwriter, playwright and actor. Self taught to read and write

Here dead we lie, because we did not choose
To live and shame the land from which we sprung;
Life, to be sure, is nothing much to lose,
But young men think it is, and we were young.

Epitaph by AE Housman (1859-1936), classical scholar and poet. Inscribed on the plaque of the British War Cemetery on Vis, an island in the Adriatic

Near this spot are deposited the remains of one who possessed Beauty without Vanity; Strength without Insolence; Courage without Ferocity, and all the Virtues of Man without his Vices. This praise, which would be unmeaning Flattery if inscribed over human ashes, is but just a tribute to the Memory of Boatswain, a Dog.

Epitaph by John Hobhouse, 1st Baron Broughton (1786-1869), Member of Parliament and author. For Lord Byron's dog Boatswain, buried in the garden of Newstead Abbey

Never say in grief that you are sorry he is gone. Rather, say in thankfulness that you are grateful he was here

Epitaph of James Mason (1909-1984), English actor. Educated at Marlborough. First in Architecture at Cambridge. Conscientious objector. Made 127 films. Author of Cats in Our Lives. Indulgent father allowing his daughter to smoke from aged three and his son to drink from aged five. Left entire estate to his second wife Clarissa who in turn, left it to her religious guru Sathya Si Baba. Buried in Vaud, Switzerland

Few thought he was even a starter.
There were many who thought themselves smarter.
Yet he ended PM, CH and OM
An Earl and a Knight of the Garter

Epitaph of Clement Atlee (1883-1967), barrister, economist, MP, Prime Minister (1945-1951). Written by himself

Without you, Heaven would be too dull to bear,
And Hell will not be Hell if you are there.

Written by Sir John Sparrow (1906-1992), Warden of All Souls,
Oxford for his friend Sir Maurice Bowra (1898-1971), classical
scholar, literary critic, academic and wit. Double First at Oxford.

1902
P.A.M
DIRAC OM
physicist
$iy\ x\ y\psi = m\psi$
1984

Paul Dirac (1902-1984), theoretical scientist, Nobel Prize winner, Order
of Merit. Refused Knighthood. "He balanced on the dizzying path between
genius and madness", Albert Einstein. (Buried in Westminster Abbey)

Love, light, peace
Duirt me leat go raibh me breoite
(I told you I was ill)

Terence 'Spike' Milligan (1918-2002), writer, artist,
musician, comedian. Milligan held an Irish passport and
the inscription is in Gaelic. St Thomas, Winchelsea

Here lies an honest lawyer
– that is Strange

Sir John Strange (1696-1754) MP, Solicitor General, Attorney General,
Privy Councillor, Master of Rolls. Rolls Chapel, now demolished

I'm a writer, but nobody's perfect

Billy Wilder (1906-2002), Austrian/American film maker, screen
writer, artist, journalist and collector. The quotation is the final
line of Some Like It Hot. Westwood Memorial Park, Los Angeles

Acknowledgements

None of the foregoing would have been possible without the dedication and perspicacity of **Lindsay Johnstone**. Accepting envelopes stuffed with assorted pieces of paper, or 'chapters' two metres long, sellotaped, stapled, handwritten, typed, printed or scribbled, she organised, interpreted, made order out of chaos and then typed out the book. Along the way, she corrected quotes in French, Greek and Latin.

To my son **Alex**, deft graphic designer and creative wizard, I owe the embellishment of this book. It might have remained mundane and soulless in its presentation had it not been for his flair for typography and artistic composition.

Kathryn Lamb first drew some cartoons for me in 1988 and she now works professionally for Private Eye, the Spectator, the Guardian and many other publications. An Oxford scholar from a distinguished diplomatic family, she is also a prolific author and illustrator of children's books. I am fortunate that she has livened up the pages of this book with her inimitable wit and precision penmanship.

The text of this book is set in Garamond Classico, a version of the Garamond typeface developed by **Franko Luin** (1941-2005), a Slovenian-Italian working in Sweden.

Claude Garamond (1480-1561), a Parisian craftsman, worked as an engraver of punches. Garamond type has spawned a number of subtle variations but fundamentally it is a Roman, upright, serif style, itself based on typefaces of the previous half century, in particular those of Venetian printer and publisher **Aldus Manutius** (1449-1515), and his punchcutter **Francesco Griffo** (1450–1518).

Lightning Source UK Ltd.
Milton Keynes UK
UKOW07f0334231217
314795UK00009BA/31/P